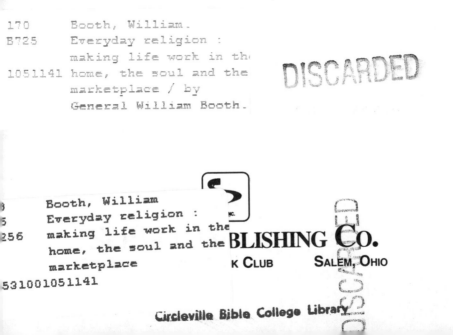

EVERYDAY RELIGION

Making Life Work in the Home, The Soul and the Marketplace

by

GENERAL WILLIAM BOOTH

BLISHING CO.

K CLUB   SALEM, OHIO

Published by Schmul Publishing Co.
PO Box 716
Salem, Ohio USA

Printed in the United States of America

ISBN 0-88019-447-2

Contents

—Part Three—

The Marketplace

—Part One—
The Home

1

Husbands and Wives Alike

ONCE BEFORE I HAVE written under this title. These chapters, I have been given to understand, have proved helpful to many of my comrades, and therefore I am encouraged to deal with other aspects of the subject. That they may prove equally useful is my earnest desire.

In commencing with a chapter that I name "Husbands and Wives Alike," I wish to make my remarks applicable to both parties in the marriage contract. And first, let me say that married life ought to be a happier and more useful form of existence than any other. Alas! I am much afraid that this is not the usual experience, and the reason why it so often falls short of the expectations commonly cherished concerning it are not far to seek. Now, I think I can give some counsels which, if followed, will help to the realization of at least a measure of the blessedness so fondly associated beforehand with matrimony, and thereby I hope to do something to make it answer the end which God had in view in its institution.

I

The Key to Happiness

1. Happiness in married life will depend with every Salvationist upon its being begun and carried on in the will of God. Remember this. If it is not of God, has not his blessing, and is not for his glory, it will come to worse than naught. But, if it is of God, it will prosper, and neither men nor devils can prevent it.

There may, and probably will be, poverty, persecution, affliction, and I know not what other tribulations associated with it sooner or later, but, if so, they will only work out the divine purpose, bring blessing to others, and eternal honor in the skies to husband and wife. See to it, therefore, that God is worshipped, feared, and obeyed, and that his approval is sought for from the beginning till the end of your union.

2. Remember, also, that happiness in the married state will be found to depend very much upon the joint performance of the duties arising out of it. The husband cannot neglect his share of the work required by the family without the wife suffering. Neither can the wife neglect her share without entailing misery on her husband. If, for instance, the husband refuses to work for the support of the household, the wife and family will starve. If the wife does not care for the home, practice economy, prepare the food, or nurse and care for the children, the husband and the whole family will suffer in consequence. And so, all the way through, both must do their part, and do it with their might.

3. Continue carefully to cherish the affection for each other already in existence. Someone has wisely said, "Be lovers still." Love is delicately constituted, and, if it is to live and thrive, it must be carefully guarded and encouraged. A great deal of the love in the married life of many dies of starvation—anyway, from neglect. If you cultivate it, you will have an abundant harvest, but if you do it violence, or even leave it untended, thorns will choke it, and it may ultimately perish.

Love—The Household's Greatest Treasure

Oh, love is the choicest treasure in your marriage outfit! All the gold and silver in the coffers of a millionaire will not purchase love, the powers of an emperor cannot win it, the learning of a scholar cannot discover it, the skill of a most inventive genius the world ever knew cannot manufacture love.

Love will make your house glad, whether it is a cottage or a mansion. Love will smooth the roughest road you may be called to travel. Love will fit your backs to whatever burden you may have mutually to bear. Love will make you equal to whatever situation you may have to fill. The love of courtship was precious to you, but the pure and mature love of marriage should be more precious still. I loved my bride before I took her to the altar, but I loved her more, and derived more happiness from my love, twenty years after that sacred event. I beseech you, take heed to your love. Encourage it, and, whatever else may come or go, do not let your love for each other fade.

4. Resolve, and hold on to your resolution, to bear and forbear with

each other's faults and infirmities. Do not be disappointed if you each find that you have not married an angel. You will have been blind indeed if you have not discerned certain failings in each other before marriage. And you will be certain to make further discoveries in the same direction as you come better to know each other.

These imperfections, whether of temper or taste, whether infirmities of body or mind, will, at the time, doubtless call for the exercise of all the patience you can command, but it must be forthcoming, or greater evils still will follow. You must cast yourself on God for the supply of all the wisdom you will need, and in nothing will he be more willing to give you an abundance of grace.

Differ, but Don't Dispute

5. You must agree to differ on small matters. Half the quarrels and divisions in married life begin with disagreements over trifles. Be content to have your own views and opinions on things that do not affect your individual consciences, or threaten to interfere with the real welfare of your family. It is sheer folly to wrangle about nothing, especially as you never know to what sad consequences such wrangling may lead.

I remember hearing of a man and his wife who, sitting at supper one evening, observed a mouse run across the floor and disappear. The husband said it ran into one hole, the wife said, "No, it ran into that," pointing to another. The husband replied that he was confident the mouse ran into the hole that he indicated, but the wife responded that she was equally confident it did not. And so the altercation went on, until it rose to high words with a bitter quarrel following, that resulted in their separation.

Seven years they lived apart, and then a reconciliation was effected, and they were happily reunited. A few days afterwards, again sitting at supper in the same room where the first dispute occurred, one of them, referring to the original quarrel, said, "But the mouse did go into that hole," and the other replied, "No, it did not," and they quarrelled again, and parted, never to be reunited in this life!

Every reader of this paper will say, "How exceedingly stupid it was to disagree over such a trivial thing!" But, are there not in many families, almost every day, misery-making differences over matters quite as unimportant. True, they may not lead to such disastrous results, but there is always the possibility of their doing so. And, even if there were no such danger, how contrary to true love, and how unlike the spirit of Jesus Christ it must be to take part in such contentions.

6. If differences should occur between you, let each be willing to bear the blame. It is not uncommon to hear the husband, under such circumstances, saying, "Well, it is all her fault," and it is not seldom that we hear the wife, in a similar manner, laying all the blame of a quarrel upon her husband.

Now, in the majority of family jars, everybody will know that there are faults on both sides. It may not be always so. I have known many wives, who for long years, have endured treatment of the most unjust and cruel character with uncomplaining patience and submission, the blame being wholly on the husband's side, and I have known husbands who have been called to suffer all sorts of wrong at the hands of their wives, without making any evil return. But, usually, although the blameworthiness may not be equally divided, some part of the fault will be traceable to both parties.

To end differences when they exist, to drive away the devil of discord as speedily as possible, and to promote concord and peace between hearts so nearly allied as are those of husband and wife, must be a truly religious duty. To attain this end, the first opportunity should be taken to effect reconciliation, and it cannot be done so quickly or so effectively in any other way as by either party finding out where he or she may have been to blame, frankly acknowledging it, and asking forgiveness for the same whether the other will do so or not.

II
Peacemaking

It is said that Mr. Wesley, on a certain occasion, had a rather serious altercation overnight with the preacher who traveled with him as his servant, in which some very high words were spoken on both sides. The next morning when they met, Mr. Wesley said, "Well, John, have you made up your mind to ask my forgiveness for what transpired last night?" John steadily said "No!" upon which Mr. Wesley responded, "Well, then, John, will you forgive me?" John immediately broke down, acknowledged wherein he had been at fault, supplicated Mr. Wesley's pardon, and they were better friends than ever.

The command of St. Paul to "Let not the sun go down upon your wrath," is peculiarly applicable to disagreements existing between husband and wife. Both should be determined never, under any circumstances, to sleep until peace is restored between them—that is, where peace is possible.

7. Endeavor to promote your partner's happiness before your own. The spirit of happiness is a precious thing in the house. Its possession permeates the amount of work performed, the lessons learned, the prayers offered, the soul-saving efforts made, and many other good services. When it is lacking in father and mother, it will very probably be absent also from the hearts of the children. Everything, therefore, should be done that can be done to create and maintain this treasure.

Much as husbands and wives have in common, they largely live separate lives. Perhaps this is true of every individual existence down here. In every breast there is a little world of responsibility, toil, anxiety, hope and fear, which is entirely its own. All of us have burdens to bear that no one else can carry for us—burdens which no one else can even share, burdens which, you might say, in all their height and depth, and length and breadth, no one but that One above can ever even know. This is particularly so with husbands and wives: consequently, each should tenderly sympathize with, and endeavor in all possible and lawful ways to comfort and cheer the other. To do this effectually let me give you the following hints.

Mutual Knowledge and Help

1. Acquaint yourselves with each other's work and difficulties. The wife should, as far as possible, live in the husband's world, interest herself in his work, acquaint herself with his difficulties, and share his hopes, so as to be able intelligently to converse with him on matters that will closely affect him, and to give him such counsel as she is able.

The husband should make himself familiar with everything of importance in his home. He should specially familiarize himself with the condition of his children, their health, their lessons, their morals, and their religion. Particularly should this interest reach out to the duties undertaken by each in connection with the corps to which they belong.

2.Find time to talk these things over together, if possible, at the end of the day. Husbands are often at fault here, I fancy. The wife's heart is frequently full of some family care, and wants to tell it out to the one dearest to her, who ought to be the one most interested, but he will often be too full of his own affairs, and too weary for anything but sleep, and so the wife must, in solitary silence, bury her care in her own breast.

Wives are often just as unwise with respect to the particular trials and anxieties of their husbands. The wife is occupied with her sewing, her children, or her housekeeping just when her husband wants to pour out the story of his trials to her, and so each is driven more or less from the other to live separate lives, to the untold loss of both, as well as the untold loss of the children.

3. Husbands and wives should practically share each other's burdens, and thereby lighten their weight, or bring strength to bear up under them. How often my dear wife used to say with a full heart, when I had acquainted her with the nature of some heavy trial, "Do this or that," at the same time giving me precious counsel, and adding, "Don't be troubled. God will carry you through." Thus the difficulty was made endurable, if it did not actually vanish away.

III
No Secrets

4. Husbands and wives should have no secrets from each other on any subject that has a connection with their well-being. An old writer protests against people carrying their hearts on their sleeves for every crow to peck at, and it certainly is not wise to do so. But this does not apply to the relations existing between married people. I advise you to lay bare your secret souls to each other when it is possible. To whom else on earth can you unburden your sorrows, tell your temptations, or describe your perplexities, so well as to each other?

5. Companion together as much as is consistent with your other duties, and so far as possible, work together in the war. How often will you see a couple who, before marriage, were scarcely ever separate, but afterwards are seldom seen together? They walk separate paths, have separate interests, and consequently, are separate in heart. This is entirely out

of harmony with the spirit of the Salvation Army.

6. As far as possible, sing each other's songs, love each other's friends, like each other's ways, cherish each other's objects, and so help to make each other strong and happy.

Mutual Responsibility

7. Realize the fact that you are to a serious extent responsible for each other's souls, and be determined to discharge your duty in this respect. I shall deal with this matter when I come to speak of the different obligations which husbands are laid under to wives, and wives to husbands, although I must just have a word or two here, namely—

a) Enquire constantly after each other's spiritual welfare. You do this with your comrades in the barracks, and when you meet them in the streets—or, if you don't, you ought to do. Then, why should you not inquire as to the religious welfare of the one who is nearer to you than any other being can be?

b) Judge each other's spiritual condition in love, but, at the same time, let it be done faithfully.

c) Pray for each other, especially pray together as well as apart.

d) Deal faithfully with each other's faults.

e) Be at trouble to instruct and cheer each other forward in a holy, self-denying life.

8. Stimulate each other's service and devotion in the Salvation War. The world is full of temptations calculated to draw one or both of you aside from making a good fight. These temptations are often described as a trinity, consisting of the world, the flesh, and the devil. Do not allow Satan to use the dearest relative on earth to steal your hearts away from that holy service and sacrifice to which you stand pledged before Heaven and earth and hell. We have already said that it is no uncommon thing for husbands and wives to become a snare to each other. But that is so important a theme that I must repeat the caution, and endeavor to give you some counsel upon it next week.

My comrades, let me ask you to take the following advice to heart and act upon it:

1. Do nothing to hinder one another from doing all that is possible to push on the War. On the contrary, unite to make opportunities for mu-

tual attendance on meetings, visitation, carrying on business, or anything else that will help the Army.

I know that this counsel applies more particularly to husbands in respect to their wives, but it will, in a thousand cases, apply to wives also with respect to their husbands. It is not an unknown thing for the wife to throw obstacles in the way of her husband doing his duty by weak and groundless fears about killing himself, and leaving her a widow and their children orphans.

2. Cheer one another forward in those hours of depression and discouragement that, with more or less frequency, come upon all the soldiers of Jesus Christ who carry the burden of souls and do their utmost to save them. The reason commonly given for marriage is the loneliness of single life and the desire for a companion who will encourage and help them to discharge the duties of life. Mind that you answer faithfully and creditably to this description of a partner.

3. Advise one another as to the real quality of the work done by each. You can point out the good parts, and you can show the imperfections of an address, or a song, or a testimony or anything else, whether sacred or secular. You are the one to suggest to the other possible improvements. Mind you do this faithfully and well. Beware of flattery. Your affection and desire to please, may tempt you in this direction.

4. Help each other in the selection of topics for your talks, lessons for your juniors, solos, and the like.

5. Help each other to keep up your family worship and to make it instructive and cheering. If your daily work keeps you away from the family altar at the hours most suitable for morning and evening prayers, find some other hour to pray daily with your children.

6. Unite in the giving of your substance to the measure of your ability.

7. Hold each other to the resolutions you have mutually formed to make your children saints and soldiers of Jesus Christ. Difficulties will be sure to arise, and temptations will cross your path in the carrying out of this purpose, and it may be that one or the other may falter in their consecration to this duty in view of the possible sacrifices involved. But you must each strive to prevent the other from going back upon the pledges made, and to be true, cost what it may, to your dedicatory vows. The children belong to God, and he must have them.

2

About Weddings

AT THE VERY GATE, as it were, of the union stands the deeply interesting ceremony of marriage itself. The old adage, "A thing well begun is half done" is certainly, to some extent, applicable to the way in which the wedding ceremony is conducted. I do not think, therefore, that a little homely advice on the manner of its performance will be out of season, or be thrown away on those of my readers who may be contemplating entering into the wedded state.

It must be remembered that I am writing to those who, I assume, have carefully weighed over and fully realized the character and consequences of the important step they are about to take, and have arrived at the conviction that they are naturally adapted to promote each other's happiness, holiness, and usefulness, and that there is a reasonable prospect of their being able to secure the temporal support required by the new circumstances which marriage will bring to them. With this assurance they may justly conclude, I think, that the proposed union will be in harmony with the will of God, and that it will secure his smile and command his blessing.

To those thus persuaded let me tender the few counsels that follow. Please bear in mind that I am writing to Salvationists:

I
Salvation in Character

1. My first counsel is, have a Salvation Army wedding. This piece of advice may at first sound unnecessary, but it is not so. Little difficulties may come in the way when you make the announcement of your intention, and friends and relatives belonging to other religious denominations, or professing no religion at all, will often oppose the idea, but you must stand firm as a rock in your determination. There

must be no compromise. Have an understanding between yourselves, and then carry it through. If people who would otherwise be present at the ceremony, or whom you would like to come, refuse to attend, you cannot help that. Tell them that, on one of the most interesting and important occasions of your life, you cannot and will not turn your back on the people who have been so frequently blessed to you, whom you have taken for better or for worse, for time and for eternity, and whom you love better than life itself.

2. Resolve that, as far as you can prevent it, none of the silly usages so commonly prevalent on such occasions shall degrade the ceremony. I do not mean that you should quarrel with friends who think that there is any practical value in scattering rice, throwing old slippers, and the like, or who imagine that such trivial customs are of service as expressing their good wishes for your future, but I do say that, as Salvationists, you should be above such foolish old wive's fables.

The same remark applies to the superstitious notions entertained by some people with regard to omens, or times and seasons. On no account would such persons be married on a Friday, while the barking of a dog, of the crowing of a cock at what they thought to be an unseasonable hour, would be regarded by them as reliable signs of "bad luck" for the future. Away with all such nonsense from the mind of the Salvationist! To him all days are good days, suitable alike for deeds worthy in themselves, and which carry with them the approbation of God and the assurance that none of the accidents of life can prevent the fulfillment of his gracious will.

A Season of Gladness

3. Determine that the ceremony itsel, and the period immediately going before and following after, shall, as far as possible, be a season of gladness. If there is any event in the natural course of a man's or a woman's life that should be bright and gladsome, surely it is the wedding day.

It is true that marriage is often the entrance to a road rougher and thornier than the one hitherto trodden, and it may bring to the shoulders of either the bride or the bridegroom a burden heavier than the one they carried when single, but then does it not also bring with it a companion who will help to smooth the rugged path, and carry the additional weight?

Marriage may, and will, bring to the heart new trials and sorrows, but they will be shared and lightened by the sympathy and fellowship of the one most beloved on earth.

Moreover, will not the changed circumstances, colored as they will be at a time like this by the excitement of the hour and novelty of the situation, promise new sources of joy and gladness in the future? Therefore banish from your minds all the little forebodings of the hour, exercise all the faith you can muster for the future, and calling together your kindred and friends, bid them be merry with you. Bring out the cornet, sound forth the durm, clash the loud timbrel, and lift up you voices to heaven in praise and thanksgiving, and while thus expressing the joy of your souls, do something towards creating gladness in the hearts of others.

Remember the Sorrowing

Salvationists are not, as a rule, able to provide expensive feasts for the poor and the needy, but to the extent of their ability, they should, on such occasions as those of which I am writing, see that some poor comrade, or some lonely widow, or some needy stranger, partakes of the crumbs that fall from their well-provided table.

That God desires the wedding day to be one of rejoicing, is plainly set forth in the numerous allusions to it in his Book.

Isaiah 62:5, "As the bridegroom rejoiceth over the bride, so shall thy God rejoice over thee."

Jeremiah 33:11, "The voice of joy and the voice of gladness, the voice of the bridegroom, and the voice of the bride."

Moreover, he uses it to illustrate the delight he experiences when he wins the souls of men and women to that perfect union with himself, which he so much desires.

4. While, however, you seek that the holy hour of your wedding day shall be bright and cheerful, beware of lightness and frivolity. Human nature, we all know, is prone to extremes, and it is in times of legitimate gladness that the temptation to foolish joking, jesting, giggling and laughter—always so unbecoming to saints and soldiers— is most likely to lead them astray. I do not know that I have ever been a witness of such levity to any serious extent, for my presence on

such occasions has always been sufficient to prevent anything of the kind happening, but I have often heard stories of giddiness and jocularity which, while not having anything actually wrong in them, have been very unlike Salvationism, and consequently have grieved me greatly. Officers and soldiers should be very careful to avoid such unseemly conduct.

Spiritual Profit

5. Arrange that the public ceremony shall, as far as possible, be the means of conveying some spiritual benefit to your own souls, and, above all, to the comrades and friends and strangers who may come to witness it. If you have accepted the principle described and laid down by the Apostle Paul, when he says, "Whether therefore ye eat or drink, or whatsoever ye do, do all to the glory of God," then this occasion, which I have shown to be one of the most interesting and important of your earthly history, ought to be so conducted, almost before all others, as to promote, in the highest degree possible, his saving purpose with regard to the perishing sons and daughters of men.

A wedding generally has an attraction for strangers and outsiders peculiar to itself. There are many people who will come to the religious ceremony connected with it who would not ordinarily cross the threshold of a Salvation barracks. See to it, therefore, that all who come to see you united shall if possible, receive some profit to their own souls in return.

II
No Vain Display

6. Avoid all vain display and unnecessary expenditure in connection with the marriage ceremony. While you should seek to provide things decent and nice in the sight of those who will be with you, do not allow your wedding to be made an occasion for transgressing those rules of simplicity, modesty, and separation from the world which you embraced when you became Salvationists. When I read the advertisements and descriptions of fashionable marriages, now so frequent, and remember how commonly they are imitated by people of the lower walks of life, I am grieved and appalled at the scandalous amount of money wasted,

and the shameful pride and vanity displayed—all of which are alas! so freely sanctioned, if not condoned by the services of religion.

Let my dear people keep as far as possible from such foolish displays of weakness and vanity, and conscientiously avoid any needless outlays of money, thereby setting the world such an example as will compel it to acknowledge the reality of your profession as meek and lowly followers of Jesus Christ. You will only accomplish this, and make the fashionable crowd wonder at and admire you, by sticking, in all thoroughness and simplicity, to your uniform.

7. Seek conversation a few days beforehand with the officer who will conduct the ceremony, and make it plain to him what your wishes are with respect to it. Give him to understand that while you desire that the service shall be conducted in the spirit of cheerfulness, at the same time you wish it to be made a means of conveying spiritual benefit to the souls of those who may attend it, and that it must not be so cheerful as to hide the importance and gravity of the event. He will most likely be of the same mind as yourself, and very pleased to know that your hearts are turned in the same direction as his own. Anyway, his hands will be strengthened by your confidence, and his soul drawn out to act in harmony with your desires.

8. Familiarize yourself with the nature of the service, and more particularly the part you will have to take in it. Consider carefully the pledges you are about to make to God and your partner on behalf of yourself and the children God may be pleased to bless you with, and pray earnestly that he will give you grace to fulfill every promise you make. By foreseeing clearly the part you will have to perform, and weighing over well what it involves, you will do much to prevent nervousness and flustration when you are publicly called upon to make those pledges of love and faithfulness required from you both.

When your turn comes to speak, say a few words in a simple, modest and earnest manner, honoring your Lord by testifying to his past goodness to you in your salvation and preservation from sin, and avow your resolution to serve him more faithfully in your new circumstances, exhorting at the same time, all present to do the same. For the ceremony to be made the occasion of the soldiers of the corps, or any considerable number of them, yielding their body, soul and spirit to the task of making themselves ready for the marriage supper of the Lamb, or of the sinners present kneeling for mercy at the Savior's feet, will be not only at the time, but forever after, a matter for deepest gratitude, increasing the glad remembrance of the hour to all concerned.

9. The same spirit which I have exhorted you to observe in the public meeting should actuate any festive gathering that may be held in connection with it. Why, my comrades, should the spirit, the consecration, and the motive which actuate us in our private festivities be any different from what they are in our public gatherings? I cannot conceive. No, the same holy, loving, blessed feelings must, on the occasions of which I am speaking, pervade our consecrations, and songs, and prayers in public as much as in private.

Take the following extract from the description of the wedding proceedings of that holy and successful soul-winner, John Fletcher, a clergyman of the Church of England, one hundred years ago.

In short, seeing that your wedding day is, as I have shown, one of the most important days of your life, you should unite yourselves together, and prevail upon as many others as will join with you, in making it a time of heavenly satisfaction and profit, not only to yourselves, but to all concerned.

10. While avoiding all undue familiarity in the presence of comrades, friends and strangers, you should, at the same time, treat each other with all the respect and affection that will be expected from you, and felt to be reasonable and proper under the circumstances, and which, if you entertain the sentiments fitted to your new relationships, you will feel to be each other's due.

11. At the end of the day, when the last hand has been shaken, and the last goodbye spoken, as you close your door upon yourselves, and you feel yourselves alone with God, ready to commence that united walk for life to which you have just pledged yourselves in the presence of your comrades, bow down together at the feet of your Heavenly Father, and unitedly give yourselves over body, soul, and spirit, together with all the possible consequences of your union, into the hands of him—your everlasting Friend.

3

About Home

FEW WORDS IN THE English language lay hold of the heart more quickly, move it more forcibly, or retain their influence over it more permanently, than the magic word, "home." How universally true of the Anglo-Saxon peoples everywhere are the oft-repeated lines:

> *Home, home, sweet, sweet home,*
> *Be it ever so humble,*
> *There's no place like home.*

To some extent this sentiment applies to the animal species as well as to the human race. The wild beasts of the forest have their particular haunts, where they hide and sleep, the birds have their favorite woods, where they sing and build their nests, the fishes have their fancied streams, which they more particularly frequent, and there is only a human being here and there who has not some spot which he dignifies with the name of home.

I
Homeless, and Why?

It is quite true that, for the good of others and the glory of his Lord, the Salvationist holds not back the pleasures of home in the consecration he makes of himself to the war, and that in practice he is often called upon entirely to forego its charms. In this he has before him the example of his Divine Master, who said of himself: "The foxes have holes, the birds of the air have nests, but the Son of Man hath not where to lay his head." In other words the Son of Man was without a home.

Thousands, at the call of the Spirit, and for the sake of a dying world, have followed the Master's example. At the head of these saints and warriors is the Apostle Paul, who gloried in being able to forego the wife, the children, and all those things which, together, constitutes the joys of home. Although they were perfectly lawful for him, he gave them up in order that he might win more souls to Christ.

The sainted and sanctified Madame Guyon expresses her conviction in the following beautiful words:

> *Thy choice and mine shall be the same,*
> *Inspirer of that holy flame*
> *Which must forever blaze!*
> *To take the cross and follow Thee*
> *Where love and duty lead, shall be*
> *My portion and my praise.*

A leading officer of the Salvation Army, on the same track, sings almost pathetically:

> *No home on earth have I,*
> *No nation owns my soul,*
> *My dwelling place is the most High—*
> *I'm under his control.*
> *No spot on earth I own.*
> *No field, no house is mine,*
> *Myself, my all, I still disown—*
> *My God, let all be Thine.*

But this dear brother has long since succumbed to the force of custom, and, although his wanderings continue, he every now and then turns his face towards home, and seeks and finds more particular rest and comfort there.

A Divine Idea

But, after all, the idea of home is a divine one. It is in the divine plan, and, therefore, in the natural course of things. The first home was in Paradise, and when expelled that blissful abode, man continued to find a home onward amongst the thorns and the thistles, and will do so, I suppose, until the end of time. God never asks for its sacrifice except some greater benefit is to be reaped by the surrender of ourselves or those about us, and even when the sacrifice has been made there will be some spot that, for the time being, will bear the endearing title of home.

Home, when it does exist, has much to do with all that concerns the highest interests of those to whom it belongs. It is ultimately associated with religion, with health, with happiness, and with usefulness, nay, it has to do with the promotion of the redeemed to Heaven.

There are many homes, alas! in this world, which may be truly described as nurseries for Hell, and which lead straight down to the bottomless pit, while there are not a few that, with equal truth, can be spoken of as training homes for the Eden above, and are like a sort of Jacob's ladder, up which fathers, mothers, children, servants, can all be seen climbing to the skies.

God's Ideal

Fathers and mothers, and those generally responsible for the wellbeing of home, should inquire before they attempt its establishment, and often pause, after it has come into existence, to ask the question, "How can we make home better answer to God's ideal?"

Let me try and point out a few things that should characterize every home, or which taken together will go to make it what God desires it to be. While beyond the reach of many soldiers in the Army, seeing that, as children, or servants, or even wives, they are powerless to control those in whose hands the government is lodged, still, my counsels will, I think, be possible of attainment to many even of the humblest of my readers, anyway, they can be aimed at, prayed for, and longed after by all.

II

1. Every home should be the dwellingplace of God. This was the chief glory of that first human home in Paradise. It was not its situation, its climate, its fruit, its flowers, or any other of its ten thousand wonders. Its chief glory, nay, the glory that eclipsed all other glories, was the fact that God was there, that he found pleasure in its occupants, and came and went with satisfaction and delight. It will be ever thus with the beautiful home on high for which we are steering.

God will be the glory of Heaven.

A Temple

To this end, every home should be definitely and truly consecrated to the service of God, as much as is the barracks. It must be a temple where he can make himself known, pour forth his Spirit, and hold communion with his children. Everything that keeps him away, or grieves him when he is there, must be put aside or never allowed to enter. I should say that this would mean no intoxicating drink, no impure literature, no foolish worldly fashion, no wasteful adornment, no injustice to the weaker members or to those who are without, no falsehood, no idleness. No, nothing should come into this home, which is God's house on earth, that you would think out of place, or unwelcome, in the mansion Jesus has prepared for you, and which you anticipate occupying in Heaven.

The Family Altar

In such a home, there will of necessity be a family altar. The first thing done by the patriarchs, when they fixed their tents, for however short a period, was to erect an altar, and offer sacrifices thereon. They thereby openly recognized the existence of Jehovah, acknowledged their dependence upon him for their every good, and gave him the worship of their hearts. Whoever would have a happy home must do the same. At stated times, morning and evening when possible, let all the members of the household gather and offer the "sacrifice" of praise and thanksgiving, interceding for the dear ones absent, the corps with which the family is connected, the Army throughout the world, and the dark, sinning multitudes around.

Daniel prayed three times a day. Is it impossible for us, in these later days, with fuller revelations and unrestricted liberty—no lions' dens staring us in the face as a penalty—to draw nigh to our Maker as frequently and as openly as did this prophet? Why not adopt some such plan for prayer as the following:

Morning—on rising: Thanksgiving for the mercies of the night and the opening day, together with reconsecration to the service of the Kingdom.

After breakfast—(1) Intercession for kindred and personal friends.

(2) For family mercies. (3) For a day of usefulness, and for God's blessing on the Salvation War throughout the whole world.

At 12:30—For soul-saving and for comrades in other countries.

Two minutes after dinner—(1) For comrades who may be sick and dying. (2) For all the saints of God everywhere.

Two minutes after tea—For the social work, the officers employed in it, and the poor everywhere.

Night—(1) Thanksgiving for the mercies of the day. (2) For the souls that have been saved. (3) For the welfare of family and friends, closing with the commendation of self, kindred and comrades to the care of the great Father.

Other objects may be added as desirable.

The Husband's Helping Hand

2. The home must be occupied by holy people. Every home should, as far as circumstances will allow, be clean. Cleanliness has been said to be next to godliness. Anyway, the two virtues are very near akin. I know how difficult it will be for many of our dear soldiers, with perhaps delicate health, large families, little or no outward help, and dwellings to which it is difficult to give even the appearance of neatness or cleanliness, to come up to their own standard in this respect. But even with these obstacles, a little contrivance and a steady aim will accomplish much. Children can be taught cleanly habits very early. Husbands who have the time should cheerfully lend a hand to the overweighed wife with the walls, ceilings, and even the floors. Why not? I can see nothing unmanly in such assistance, and I can see a great deal that is very humane—nay, I might say, very Christlike.

To those in whose way no such difficulties as I have mentioned lie, cleanliness is an absolute duty. Without it they will be a disgrace to themselves, the Army, their children, and do what may prevent home happiness altogether. Of course, keeping things clean will occupy a good deal of time which, perhaps, they would like to spend in doing good to the bodies and souls of those about them. But let them be careful not to encumber themselves with things which can be done without, but which will require a deal of time and labor to keep clean.

4

About Husbands: Their Privileges and Duties

A LITTLE CAREFUL OBSERVATION of men and things will show, I think, that every station in life, when rightly filled, carries with it certain advantages peculiar to itself which cannot otherwise be gained. For instance, the privileges, possessions, and special opportunities connected with the position of a ruler are not shared by those he governs, while, on the other hand, the governed have certain advantages and pleasures not possessed by a ruler.

The principle suggested by this contrast applies to the important position occupied by a husband. His is no exception to the general rule. And yet these advantages are not always recognized by those concerned, and it is, I think, very desirable that some of them should engage our attention. Last chapter, my readers will remember that I closed my remarks on the equality of husbands and wives. This week I begin the consideration of the privileges and duties of husbands, and I start by pointing out:

I
A Divine State

That one great benefit conferred by the marriage state is the realization of that highest form of human affection, namely the acquisition of a lifelong friend, a kindred soul.

The majority of us know something of the pleasures and benefits flowing out of pure and disinterested friendship. The communion of heart and soul that marked the relation of David and Jonathan has been the admiration of the world from their day to ours. But, when found in the union of husband and wife, the benefits derived from a friendship based on, and characterized by, the same exalted qualities, far exceed any that can spring from a close fellowship existing between man and man. The married state, if rightly discharged, is the highest form of friendship. It is divine!

In view of my own experience in the long companionship of my precious wife, I must confess that I can scarcely trust myself to discuss this subject. It recalls memories which overwhelm my feelings, but I will endeavor to write soberly and practically, not going beyond the region of what can be attained in the experience of those for whose help and blessing these papers are intended.

Solomon says, "Whoso findeth a wife findeth a good thing." The word "thing" should not have been introduced into the passage. The meaning is complete without it. A true wife is a "good," and a good in the fullest sense of the word.

The felicity of such a companionship may not, I admit, always be attained in all its possible and desired degree. Dissimilarity of tastes, or disposition, or opinions, will effectually prevent this, and two souls, while occupying the same home, sitting at the same table, being the parents of the same children, may be as far apart as the poles are asunder as regards that higher inward life.

Division

This division may, in ten thousand cases, be accounted for by the fact that the necessity of such agreement of heart and soul was never fairly recognized by the parties when marriage was first contemplated. Indeed, there was not even the thought, much less the expectation, of such a unity, so that there is no just room for complaint if it does not exist.

In other cases, one view on such matters of everlasting importance as conversion, will be held by one party and rejected by the other, so that both are condemned to walk a lone path, thus marring their happiness and welfare for time and eternity. This, again, gives little cause for a murmuring thought, because, in such a case, the answer would be, "If in the days of thy youth thou hadst chosen thy Maker for thy husband, and walked consistently with his wishes, a partner after thine own heart might have been thy portion, anyway, this source of sorrow would not have arisen."

But when a husband does find this unity of thought, feeling, and purpose in a wife, what a treasure he has obtained, and how proud and thankful ought he to be for the prize!

Among her qualities, please let all husbands note the following:

1. The man who finds such a wife, finds a friend to whose bosom he can unreservedly confide all the secrets of his soul. Every husband will have his trials. In the world he will have tribulations—and especially will this be the case if he is an out-and-out Salvationist—and it will always bring him a measure of relief to tell out the things he suffers into a sympathetic ear. A verse of a quaint old song expressing this sentiment has often proved helpful in my experience:

> *What is it that casts you down?*
> *Who are they that grieve you?*
> *Speak and let your wants be known,*
> *Speaking will relieve you.*

The Wife's Heart

Every man has some particular difficulties that trouble him more than others, and which he cannot, with any degree of confidence, explain even to an ordinary friend. Perhaps it will be a mistake he has made, a temptation that harasses him, a besetting sin to which he has yielded, or, it may be something that troubles his conscience or lies heavy on his heart, and which his whole nature shrinks from asking counsel upon or confessing to any living creature, excepting one. There is one ear that will ever be ready patiently to hearken to the story of his sorrows, and one heart that will ever sympathize with him—that ear and that heart are owned by his wife. To her he can confide those secret infirmities and shortcomings of heart and life which he would not dare to unfold to the cold world around him. He has no anxiety of her doing any other than hiding the things that he would himself cover up, or of helping to bear the burden he has to carry.

This is the natural outcome of the union. They are no longer two souls, but one, and not only does the wife expect to share her husband's goods and possessions, whether they are many or few, but she rejoices to share the trials of his life and the sorrows of his heart. Now, who can possibly estimate the value of the treasure such a wife must be?

The Husband's Chaplain

2. The husband will find in a true wife, a spiritual director and guide. She will be the chaplain of his soul. A great deal has been said on the value of the confessional as used in the Catholic church, and, beyond question, the privilege of acknowledging and mourning over the sins of the past, and receiving spiritual counsel with respect to them from those whose wisdom and confidence can be trusted, is an undoubted help. But the terrible abuses with which the practice has been attended, and the horrible evils to which it has led, have caused a large part of the Christian church, not only to avoid but execrate it. Still, when a man has some sin upon his conscience, or some evil besetment that has mastered him, or temptation that he hates, yet feels as though it were impossible to resist, what is so natural as that he should yearn to confide it all to someone on whom he can rely?

Now, there will be in every corps men who will gladly listen to such trying experiences on the part of the men, and women on the part of the women, but the husband who has a true wife need go no further for such assistance than his own chamber, nor seek for any other confessor than her to listen to the story of his trials.

Such a wife as I shall attempt to describe in the course of the following papers will be admirably fitted for the task. She knows her husband, is familiar with his weaknesses and dangers, she loves his soul, and is interested, before all others, in his fidelity to truth, and duty and God. She can afford to be fearless, and, with every instinct of her nature, she ought to tell him the truth. Alas! while I write, I feel that I am open to the enquiry, "Is this the usual treatment that wives deal out to their husbands?" and I am compelled to make the reply, "I fear not."

II

3. The husband will find in such a wife as I have previously described a genuine comforter in all his sorrows. When other hearts grow cold, and other sympathies are withdrawn, when old comrades turn away their faces from him, and old helpers withdraw their generous hands, her heart will beat the faster, and creep up the closer,

and her arms will cling the tighter in holding him up while undergoing the rougher experiences of life.

4. The husband will, as far as possible, share with his wife every form of gladness which falls to his lot. I can truthfully say that I never tasted what was pleasant to my palate, never saw a sight of beauty in art or nature, never heard a sound of melody in music or song, never experienced a joy in friendship, never had a triumph in my work or welfare— nay, I can go further, and say that I never had a heavenly manifestation to my soul, without desiring my dear wife to share it.

And there was nothing singular in my experience. It is perfectly common to husbands, I am happy to say, and no particular credit is due to them, either, on that account, for where true love—that is, real oneness—exists, this sharing of pleasant things means the doubling, nay, the trebling, of these treasures. While all true love would fain screen the object of its affection from sorrow, and longs to bear every grief on its behalf, it cares for no gladness that its object cannot know and share, so that, in a wife a husband finds the means for the manifold multiplication of his joys.

5. A true husband will find in a true wife a faithful advisor in his perplexities. Oh, how little do men dream of the valuable counsel of which they deprive themselves in failing to make their wives, as far as possible, their confidants in all matters of perplexity! It is quite true that, in the Salvation Army, the views taken of woman's capacities and position render the observations made here and elsewhere in these papers of less importance than they would otherwise be. Still, I am afraid that the foolish, unscriptural, and irrational notions about woman's natural inferiority have not been utterly extirpated from the hearts of all who are marching under our flag.

A woman is, in many respects, remarkably able to advise her husband on the bewildering secular matters with which he is ever called to deal, and, if he will give the chance she will show this ability with no inconsiderable advantage to him.

Outside our ranks, this chance is commonly denied her, for in too many cases she is regarded by her husband as only a kind of toy, to minister to his amusement; or as a mother, to nurse his children and look after their needs; or as a housewife, to see to his eatings, and drinkings, and clothing. Beyond this, he sees no end that a wife can serve. Hence, he keeps her in ignorance of the busy world in which he lives and moves. If, however, the husband will condescend to acquaint the wife with the doctrines and duties of his religion, with the ins and outs of his business, with the character of the men who move in the circle of his acquaintance, and the host of things that occupy him day after day, he will often find her better able to advise him to his good than the ordinary run of people whom he consults when beset by trials and burdened by care.

A woman will often look at matters from a different standpoint to that taken by men. She will judge things, as we sometimes say, by her instinct, which will often simply be a keener sense of right and wrong than that possessed by men, combined with a greater readiness to face the difficulty of the present hour, although it may involve the sacrifice of a lesser gain to compass a greater future good. In other words, the true woman will care less for consequences and more for what is right.

Men are more given to look at things from the standpoint of expediency than are women, and I am sure their training and intercourse with society makes them more timid about consequences. Perhaps it is because they see further into the future, or it may be a sense of responsibility for their families and their fellows makes them fearful of taking courses which they conceive to be the best, and which otherwise they would choose to follow.

6. In a wife a man finds a true partner in all his earthly interests. It is true that, ordinarily, she will bring with her the occasion for increased financial responsibilities, but this will probably prove to him a profitable part of the discipline of life, by strengthening and deepening his nature as nothing else will.

Men are naturally more selfish than women, and their meanness will grow and thrive every day they live upon the earth if there is nothing to call forth their generosity.

In well-assorted and prudent marriages, it is strange how the income will keep pace with the expenditure. I should think, if an enquiry could be made upon the subject, it would be found that in most cases the married man, with wife and children to support, finds himself better off, and with more home-comforts, than he would have been had he remained single. The income, as by providential arrangement, wonderfully keeps pace with the outlay.

I have heard the poor peasant people in England say, when the sixth or seventh accession has been made to the family, without any apparent increase in the means of supplying its wants, "Oh, sir, God never sends little mouths without something to fill them!" If this sort of argument applies to the arrival of a child in a home, how doubly applicable it must be to the advent of a wife! She comes at once to relieve home of the labor of the hireling, and to manage her husband's earnings with strictest economy, it being her own things and not those of a stranger of which she ministers. She comes not to measure her time, nor strength, nor gifts, nor anything else she possesses—she lays her all at his feet, and then toils for them as diligently and as skillfully as she would toil for her own.

III

7. The husband finds in a good wife the completion of his own character. Humanly speaking, he is an unfinished, imperfect creature until he finds a wife and educates his heart. She is the second and brighter side to him; she completes his natural education of heart, making a more manly man of him.

In saying this, and in much that has gone before, and also in much that will follow after, I am in danger of being a little misunderstood, but you must remember that I do not write for those who are perfect, and that I am not attempting to describe the exceptions in life. I have no doubt about Paul's doctrines, and endorse with all my heart his declaration that in certain states a single life, when it can be accepted by man, offers more facilities for the service of God, and that a man unencumbered with wife and family will be at an advantage in the Salvation War over one with them.

I was reading a little time back how that in the French and German war, when the *Landwehr*—that is, the soldiers who had been called up from their homes to fight—were ordered forward to meet the enemy, it was a common thing to see them, strong and brave as they were, burst into tears and faced the storm of shot and shell sobbing with emotion. The youngest recruits of yesterday plunged into the fight with shouts and songs, apparently without a thought of what might befall them. How was this? The explanation is easily found. The elder men were husbands and fathers, and, knowing that some of them had to fall, they wept in anticipation over the desolation which they knew their death or wounds would bring to those who were dependent upon them for food, and raiment, and all the natural joys of life. With the younger men there was no such call made upon their sympathies, and, with free and unburdened hearts, careless about themselves, they fought their fight.

Even so with the soldier of Jesus Christ. The man (or the woman) who is unmarried is free to go to war or stay. His absence means no one's hurt, his death leaves none homeless and desolate, and there is no question but that if he can so far manage his heart and body as to be free in spirit for this whole-soul service of his Lord, it is best for the kingdom of Heaven, and not any worse for him.

8. A wife brings to her husband those innocent pleasures and recreations that come from the possession of a family. The desire in men for children, while not so absorbing as in women, exists. No sooner is marriage decided upon than the yearning for children springs up, and the husband's mind is filled with pictures of the pleasure he will reap from their society, and the profit which in the future they may bring him in business, and the credit they may bring him with the little world in which he moves, for in proportion as a wife loves her offspring, a husband may be said to be proud of them.

The Salvationist, in addition to the motives already referred to, hails his sons and daughters as so many reinforcements for the Army and his King, and counts them as soldiers as soon as they have commenced to breathe the vital air.

I was talking one night to an electrician about his soul on board a vessel in which I was voyaging. He had told me before that he had three little boys, and I wanted to know what would become of them if their father died. He knew very little English, and I knew less German, and so I don't think he understood me, for he replied, "Oh, the Kaiser will provide for my three boys in his army or his navy!" That was his idea about the future of his boys. They must go to fight for the emperor and the fatherland. And he regarded the prospect with satisfaction. So, every good Salvationist will, I think, with intelligent pleasure, rejoice over his children as being recruits for the great Army of the King of kings.

9. A wife will bring her husband the joys of home life. Everybody sings "Home, home, sweet home," and home is not only worth singing about, but valuing highly, both as being the dwelling-place of the purest pleasures of human life and as the nursery where some of its loveliest virtues are brought into being and trained up to maturity. How much Great Britain owes to its love and culture of home-life will never be known in this world.

Such a home makes man the better,
Sweet and lasting its control;
Home, with pure and bright surroundings,
Leaves an impress on the soul.

But no man can be said to have a home, in the highest sense of the word, without a wife. That does not say that no man will be happy unmarried. Happiness depends on the possession of a clean heart, faithfulness to right principles, and his devotion to the service of God and man. Indeed, as experience teaches, God can make his joy to abound in the soul of a true soldier under any circumstances, while, as Paul affirms, and as we have just observed, the opportunities for usefulness may be even greater in a single than a married state.

Still, I write for everyday people and the conditions of ordinary life. I say that marriage is of divine appointment, and amongst other blessings brought to a husband by a good, faithful, and affectionate wife, will be the happy home which, in many respects, comes far on for being the truest type of the heavenly rest.

It is quite true that many of the advantages I have endeavored to set forth, as possessed by the husband in the married state, may be very imperfectly realized. The wife in herself, and in the discharge of her duties, may come far short of what I have tried to picture, but even then the man generally has much, very much, to be thankful for. Often this will be only imperfectly prized, often not prized at all, until forfeited and lost forever by death. Then its value may come to be appreciated—perhaps not then!

IV
Responsibilities

The advantages enjoyed in every position carry with them responsibilities. By responsibilities it will be known that I mean the obligation to discharge certain duties. It is right that it should be so. Man was not created merely for enjoyment, but for work. God expects that he shall give as well as receive. It was so from the beginning. Man was put down in the garden with the privilege of eating and drinking, sleeping and loving; but, at the same time, he was enjoined to cultivate the garden, and obey and worship his Maker. Both principles have to do with the making of character, which is only saying that the discharge of his duties here will qualify him for higher, grander work up yonder, and the enjoyment of far more glorious bliss.

Anyway, the two go together. They cannot be separated in the relationships that we are discussing. The husband cannot, must not, expect to have all the privileges of married life without paying the price—that is, without discharging the obligations connected with the position. If he does, he will be grievously disappointed, and spoil his lot into the bargain, for verily, verily, many a marriage union, commenced under the sunniest auspices, has been marred on this account. The wife has brought to the altar, and to the home, the deepest, tenderest affection, and the determination to do all that in her lies to make that husband and that home happy and good, but the cold and thoughtless neglect of her feelings and interests has gradually soured her disposition, weaned her heart from its old affection, and made her careless about her duties, while life itself has been made, on both sides, a burden and a shame.

The Husband's Headship

Now, let me look at some of the duties for which, it seems to me, the husband is responsible:

The husband is responsible for the general well-being of the home and all therein. He is the head of the house, the wife and the children. The interests of an army necessitate a general; of a ship, a captain; of a family, a head. The husband is that head. Nothing that he can do can relieve him from that responsibility so long as he lives. It is his work to see that a home is provided, food supplied, and everything necessary to the life and health of all that are under his roof procured.

This headship also carries with it the responsibility for defense in any and every serious peril, whether from disease, robbers, or enemies of any kind. The wife and children, and all within his walls, instinctively turn to him in times of danger. If he is captain he must be the first to meet the foe and the last to leave the ship. "The women and the children first," expresses the chivalry of the true husband's heart. There is no getting away from this doctrine. It is the law existing all through the natural world, and it is the law laid down in the Bible from beginning to end, not only by command, but by example.

It is a law of necessity. Two cannot walk together except they are agreed. But, as it is impossible—anyway, very improbable—that two should always agree on every question of conduct, and if there is to be uniform harmony between them, they must agree, in the case of such differences, to accept the decision of both, and act according to it. In this case the law of Scripture, and of usage, and of common instinct, points to the husband as that one.

Perfect Union Possible

Here I may be asked, "What about the oneness of the union previously referred to, and equally asserted by the Bible, as existing between husband and wife?" I reply that there is nothing in this headship to prevent the most perfect union between the two. When a husband is prepared to confer with his wife on all matters in which she feels any interest, and of which she has any knowledge, and is willing to accept and act upon her judgment when he has reason to believe that it is more intelligent and reliable than his own, and when the wife acts towards the husband in the same spirit, it will be found, I think, that the headship is little more than a nominal one, and that for all practical purposes they are as one soul.

The husband will gradually grow prouder of his wife's capacity, and find the use of it more to his profit, and the wife will gradually acquire more and more confidence in her husband's judgment, and find more satisfaction in relying upon it. There will be no petty jealousies on the part of the husband as to the wife intruding herself on his sphere of action, and far from any mortifying sense of domination being experienced by the wife as to the headship of her husband, the danger will all be in the opposite direction. For when a woman is conscious that she possesses the love of a husband, who daily gives her the respect and devotion which are her due, and who, she believes, would willingly lay down his life in her defense—even as Christ loved and gave his life for the church—she will be in danger of going to the extreme in her obedience.

IV

2. The husband is responsible for the supply of the temporal needs of his household. When he took upon him the high responsibility of leading his wife to the altar, and, if possible, the greater responsibility still of the paternity of her children, he assumed the sacred duty of supplying their need. It is true that his wife will commonly be ready enough to join hands with him in doing her share towards the maintenance of the flock, but while he has health and strength nothing will relieve him from the main responsibility in the matter. In writing for Salvationists I have no need to talk about the heartless shamefacedness with which any number of fathers, calling themselves men, walk about the earth in debauchery and idleness, while their children are crying for bread, or at least living without the necessaries of daily life, than which I know of nothing much more mean and cowardly except it be the beggarly excuses made for such conduct.

3. The husband is responsible for the continued and careful cherishing of his love for his wife. Now, I have already dwelt at some length upon this topic in my first chapter. Still, it is so vital a point that I must be allowed to say something further concerning it. Love is ever and everywhere counted a precious thing. The affection existing between man and wife before marriage is celebrated without end, forming the favorite and most popular subject for painting, music, and song. Love after marriage, however, is but little talked about, in fact, scarcely ever mentioned. According to the painter, the poet, the novelist and kindred authorities, Cupid, the fabled god of love, takes little notice of lovers after they have been fettered by the bonds of wedlock, except, alas! it be in the case of illicit affection, which, to their shame be it spoken, constitutes a theme of

undying interest both to the authors and readers of fiction.

And yet I defy all the authors and observers of human nature in the wide world to produce examples of purer, more satisfying, and soul-exhilarating affection than can be found in the privacy of married life. The poet Cowper writes of such a union as follows:

> *Domestic happiness, thou only bliss*
> *Of paradise that has survived the fall.*

On this matter, let me give a testimony. I am ever referring to my own experience, and that partly because it is my own, and can, therefore, be referred to with confidence. I loved as lovers love for three long years before it was my privilege to take my beloved from her father's house, and call her by the precious name of wife. I loved her, I repeat, before that time. My nature is not without a measure of those powers of imagination and airy castle-building which, together, help so much to constitute the pleasure and romance of courtship, so that I know something of the love which precedes the altar. But I can testify that the love of the gloomiest and stormiest days with which our married career was so frequently checkered—even the day when I saw her fading as a fair flower and dying before my eyes—excelled in force and fervor anything and everything that went before.

The husband should cherish his love because it will so often prove the only means of retaining the love of his wife. It is true that woman's heart, in thousands of instances, continues to beat true, though called to suffer the bitterest knowledge that can ever come to a wife, namely, that her husband has turned away from her and is now given to money, or business, or politics, or public affairs, or perhaps what will be to her the lowest depth of agony—a strange woman. In such a case, is it to be wondered at if the wife's affections dry up, and her heart looks elsewhere for the responsive endearment and fellowship which is denied her at its legitimate source? Forsaken, betrayed, and neglected, is it surprising that she should go into this affection business on her own account, and find, or try to find, the heaven denied her in her husband's bosom in her children and acquaintances, or that she should go further afield still, or that she should even sink down into the regions of profligacy, or that she should slowly pine away and die of a broken heart? On many a wife's grave might be truthfully written—"I died for want of love promised me by my husband at the altar."

V
Equality

4. The husband must regard his wife as a being of equal value with himself, and treat her accordingly. The difficulties which numbers of husbands experience commence in their intercourse with their wives. They don't accept the real equality of the woman with themselves. They are taught the contrary from their youth up. They learn it from servants, and sometimes silly mothers will convey the idea, by their partiality and by more favored education and attention, that boys are superior to girls. The idea is commonly seconded by companions at school, in the playground, and openly asserted by their associates in after life. Unfortunately, the women accept the idea because they do not know better, or because of their natural meekness, or to please and curry favor with the men, and so married life begins by basing itself on this fallacy.

It is a fraud perpetrated on the sex, and works badly. Many a woman in her secret soul knows that, although she may be different from her husband and inferior to him, in some particulars, she is as good a being as he is, and perhaps, in the nobler traits of character, vastly his superior, yet she has to submit to his domination on this false and hollow plea.

A wife may, and often, as we have said, does, differ very widely from her husband, but differing, as she may do, in some particular faculties does not necessarily imply inferiority as a whole. Do not men differ from men? Will any two men whom you meet as you pass along the city street be alike in body, mind, and brain? Of course not. But no one argues that this difference supposes that one part of the people must be inferior beings to the other. The difference between husband and wife will not be greater than that which we usually find in men.

Some Differences

There are differences, of course, between the man and the wife. For instance, the husband will ordinarily excel the wife in physical force. He will beat her at filling a coal wagon, digging a hole, or rowing a boat. He has more power to endure cold or heat, and, I was going to say, to suffer pain, but if I had made the latter statement it would certainly have been a mistake, for in this respect woman is unquestionably his master, and even his superiority in some of the physical faculties we have noticed is largely the result of training and exercise.

The husband will occasionally excel the wife mentally or emotionally, but here, again, superiority in these faculties does not prove her to be an inferior being. On the contrary, go back to the beginning and give her the same opportunities as he has had and she will not be far behind even in these respects. Anyway, I am prepared to contend that, take her altogether, when she has a cell less in her brain than her husband she will have a fiber more in her heart, and when she has a fiber less in her heart you will find that she has a cell more in her brain.

Now, I urge husbands to avoid making a wrong start on this question, and then they will avoid the mistake in the intercourse that follows. Say to your wife, "Now, then, come, we will start fair. Ours is an equal partnership. We will go in for equally sharing the duties and responsibilities of our position, as we are equally constituted for filling our own particular part."

Keeping Up the Little Attentions

5. The husband is responsible for giving his wife, in the home, a position answering to this equality. He should be at some trouble to pay her a respect worthy of the relations in which she stands to him. If she is a part of him, let him treat her as he would like others to treat him. He should be careful to keep up all those little attentions with which he was proud to favor her before marriage. Then he was ever ready to run, and fetch, and carry for her. Whether it was the cloak she had left upstairs, or the book that she had lost, or the paper that had slipped from her fingers, he was there ready and willing to minister to her in these attentions, which, while seemingly trifling in themselves, nevertheless had much to do with the affections she returned and the respect in which she was held by those round about. If those attentions were good then, they are equally so today. Do not stop until moved by some involuntary impulse to render them. Make it your duty, however you may feel about them, and it will become your pleasure in the long run. And when the family comes

along, such respectful treatment will tell upon them. The rude, familiar treatment which some children render to their mother disgusts me when I am called to witness it, not only from a feeling of sympathy with the pain it must continually inflict upon her, but as indicating what may be expected, with interest, from them in after years.

While for this I am aware that the indulgent mother will often be largely to blame, yet I am equally sure that it can as frequently be traced to the husband himself. The children note the father's gruffness and the want of those little compliments in his dealings with their mother that would make it almost as pleasant for her to serve as to be served, and are ready enough to imitate him.

Alas! how common it is to hear a father all honey and smiles in his conversation with the stranger within his gates, expending on him an overflowing amount of grateful acknowledgment for any trifling favors, while he allows his wife to toil for his comfort from morn till night without once saying, "If you please," or "Thank you." Such seed-sowing in their presence is sure to produce a harvest of discord, sorrow, and in some cases the total decline of all heart affection for one another, and in others separation.

VI

6. The husband must specially care for the temporal comfort and bodily needs of his wife. This might be taken as being included in what we have already said about the husband's responsibility for the family need, but a word or two further with special reference to the wife will not, I think, be considered unnecessary. The sacrificing character of woman has been referred to before in these papers, and will probably be mentioned again. Of this the husband should take careful note, and be mindful. He should remember, all the way through, that because she does not complain it does not follow that she does not suffer.

The Pearl of Kindness

The husband ought to make it law to himself to show his wife uniform and persevering consideration and kindness. Kindness is duty readily understood, easily performed, costs very little, and yet is among the most useful and highly-prized graces that any man can practice. Especially will it shine, and particularly will it be found useful, in the relations existing between husband and wife. A man may not be able to give the partner of his joys and sorrows much money for housekeeping, or place her in any high position in society, or provide her a comfortable home, or bestow upon her the luxuries that other women in her circle enjoy, but he can constantly give her those gentle and untiring attentions which spring from a heart of kindness.

The Wife's Health

This feeling will lead him: (a) To seek to form, and ever bear in mind, a correct idea as to her health. The self-sacrificing spirit before referred to, and the desire to spare the husband anxiety, taken together with the natural buoyancy of spirit possessed by many women, lead them to conceal their pains and maladies from their partners. Many a precious woman, with a hidden disease, who might have been saved had some anxious eyes only discovered the secret enemy at an earlier date, travels too far on the road to the dark grave for medical skill or nursing care to be of any avail. It is one of the husband's first duties to get a general idea of the constitution of his wife, carefully including such disease, or tendency to disease, as she, unfortunately, may have already developed, and to do it with as much thoughtful care as he would were it his own case he was considering. Did he not promise, in the most solemn manner, at the altar, to " . . . have and to hold from this day forward, for better, for worse, for richer, for poorer, in sickness, and in health, to love, and to cherish, till death us do part?" And how can he cherish and ward off the evils that beset her without a knowledge of the same? A thoughtful husband will be the wife's best and most trustworthy physician, and ought to be the most successful in keeping off the foe, always remembering that "prevention is better than cure."

The Wife's Work

(b) This kindness will lead the husband to be considerate as to the character of the work that falls to a wife's lot, and the hours she is engaged upon it. It will be generally known that I am a believer in hard work, and that for both sexes alike. As a rule, the husband will belong to "the horny-handed sons of toil," and if he acts upon the advice already given in these papers, the amount of work he seeks to perform will only be bounded by his ability. The same rule will apply to his wife. There is no room for what may be styled "Ladyism"—taken to signify "Donothingism"—in the circle for whom I prescribe. Let it be understood that the wife must work, and work hard, and, if needs be, work in the field or the garden. Why not? Is there anything more undignified or unhealthy in a woman helping her husband to put in the seed, or reap the crop, or help her fisher-husband to pull home the boats, under the fair sunshine, and breathing God's pure, beautiful air, than, to stand many weary hours in a stifling atmosphere following the monotonous and uninteresting task of minding a machine?

But I leave that. I have been saying that I am not opposed to the wife's working. Excepting in circumstances of necessity, she will usually find her work in her own home and with her own children. That will make sufficient demands upon her energies, and occupy a fair share of her time, and when her gifts point out higher duties still, then by all means let her have help with the scrubbing of the floors, the minding of the children, and the mending of the clothing, and go forth to labor in the still more important work of caring for the sick, the dying, and the lost.

But I am wandering away from the point at which I started, which was that whatever work the wife had, by providence, or ability, or opportunity devolved upon her, the husband is responsible for not allowing her to go beyond her strength. According to the apostle, God has made him the master of her body. "For the husband is the head of the wife, even as Christ is the head of the church." (Ephesians 5:23) He sought it, and she gave it to him, and he will be a traitor to the precious trust if he does not guard the treasure and see that, in her generous concern for his needs, and those who belong to him, she does not overtax her strength, and thereby do herself lasting harm.

The Danger of Hurry and Scurry

It is not so much the work as the long hours, I fancy, on which the poor man's wife is likely to go astray. When the little children come along quickly, with their teething and other troubles, endless in number and wonderful in variety; when the husband is sick, and other trials overtake the household, the wife, by losing her natural rest, and the scurry and flurry in which these anxieties keep her night and day, is in danger of undermining what may be naturally a strong constitution, or to bend the bruised reed too far for it ever to stand up again.

Husbands will often have employments or engagements that will so far tax their energy by day as to make it difficult, if not impossible, for them to share the night watchings and service required in the sicknesses that, alas! are not uncommon in the family household. When, however, it is possible, it will be very unhusbandly, to use a very mild term for the description of this conduct, if they do not cheerfully insist on taking turn and turn about on such occasions, and even when they can not render such substantial assistance to their poor and over-burdened helpmeets, they will render what service they can.

Of course, there is an alternative I have not mentioned that will go far to meet the difficulty, and that is the hiring of the services of strangers to give the required assistance. This, however, will not be always within the ability of the class for whom I am writing. When it is, it should be done. I have known husbands who have allowed willing wives to destroy health and life rather than spare out of their savings wherewith to provide the needed help. The spirit imparted by Salvationism will render such conduct impossible I hope. Anyway, to be forewarned is to be forearmed, and the husband who wants to fulfill his pledge, and keep the mother of his children at her post, will be watchful that she does not permanently damage herself by her exhausting toil.

VII

(c) The kind husband will be careful that his wife has, as far as he can command it, a sufficient quantity of nourishing food. This suggestion may appear rather trivial, but my own observations go to show that it is needed.

I fancy that many wives, out of the kindliness of their disposition, and the notion that men require much better support both in quality and quantity than women, are ever in the habit of giving them the lion's share of such good things as come within their ability, and it may be, and probably is, largely the result of want of thought rather than the want of a chivalrous, generous disposition, that the husbands are perfectly willing to receive such favor.

Now, I do not object to the wife providing the best things for her husband—it is just like her to do so, but I do object to the husband accepting them without inquiring or considering what sort of a supply is left for the wife. If I were a husband, I should object to feasting on the one chop on the table, and leaving to my beloved some scraps gathered, say, from the former day's meal. And especially would this be the case if she were at the time supplying vital force to a baby boy or girl.

Let your love be sufficiently practical to care for these everyday necessities of your partner. You do not consider it beyond you to ask with interest the question, "What have you got for my dinner?" Exercise as much curiosity as to the provision for your wife, and see that she has the choicest share of it when the meal does come forth.

The Husband and Sickness

(d) The husband should get to know, at the earliest opportunity, the nature of the malady. A doctor may be useful for this purpose. In many diseases to which women are most subject, the opinion of a practiced nurse may be necessary. Especially would I recommend such an inquiry if a Salvation Army nurse is within reach. Anyway, heaven and earth should be moved, the one by prayer, and the other by inquiry, until you have got to know what the disease is from which the wife is suffering. That ascertained, act according to the best light you have, and the best advice, medical or otherwise, you can obtain. I only give one counsel. Beware of quackery. Have nothing to do with medicines that profess to cure all the diseases that flesh is heir to.

(e) Take an interest in the sickness, and let your wife see that you do. Your sympathies will do more for her than the choicest physic that can be found.

(f) Devote what time to her bedside your daily toil and other duties will allow. The leisure hours of Salvationists are busily occupied, and a good wife will not desire you to neglect your work in the corps and outside of it to sit by her. Still, you will be able to find supplies now and then, so as to enable you to make her feel that she still lives in your heart. Satisfy her of that, and it will go far to help her to live to serve you and the kingdom another day, or to die in peace and to leave behind her best blessing for you and for your children.

A New Husband and Father

7. The husband should share the family cares of his wife. I cannot help feeling that I am here and there repeating myself. Perhaps I may, to some extent, be referring to duties that are of a somewhat similar nature, but the reader must remember that I write for those who have not had a very careful training in such matters—indeed, for many who never knew what family love was before their conversion. Take, for instance, the testimony of a man who was brought under my notice by a dear officer a little time back. The speaker was some fifty years of age: "Speak not a word agin the Salvation Army," said he. (It was in the open air that some chaff was being rather freely indulged in on that ever-interesting theme.)

"Speak not agin the Salvation Army. Before I came under its influence I was a drunkard. I was never properly sober for twenty years. It was late at night when God met and converted my soul, and I should think it was near midnight when I got home. My wife trembled when she heard my step on the stair. She expected oaths, and perhaps blows—as was the custom in those days. But I rushed into the room, and, to her amazement, flung my arms around her neck and said, 'Wife, a husband has come home tonight!' and then kissed her. I had never done that sort of thing since we were married, twenty years before. I then said, 'Where are the children?' and I had them all out of their beds of rags and straw, and I said to them, 'You have got a father now,' and then I kissed them, and I declare to you that I had never kissed them before since they were born. Friends," said he, "never say anything agin the Salvation Army! It did that for me, and I have stood to it."

Now, when I write, for at least many of this class, I feel that I cannot speak too plainly—no, not plain enough, and I cannot very well go over the ground too often. Those who want the information put differently must go elsewhere.

Now, as I was saying that the husband must join with his wife in the cares ever connected with family and home. On the wife the lion's share of this burden must necessarily rest. It is true that the man has, in many cases, to go forth to meet dangers by land and perils by sea, in order to earn the family's daily bread. He leaves the wife all snug and comfortable in her cozy home, while he risks life and limb in the battle with machinery above ground, or the fire-damp below, and a thousand other foes to health, comfort, and life itself.

Little Things

Still, with all these perils and inconveniences, a certain amount of excitement is associated, which will often make the life easier to bear than the monotonous, lonely duty that a woman has to endure. Now, a husband ought, I think, to bear this in mind, and to remember also that with her life there are associated a certain number of little, trying cares, of which she can speak to no one so readily as to him, and on no one has she anything like so strong a claim for sympathy and counsel. It is not uncommon, I imagine, for husbands to regard their family as matters of small moment. The sicknesses, accidents, naughtinesses and education of the children; the waywardness of servants, when such luxuries are kept; the care of the house, the awkwardness of the tradespeople, the exactions of relatives, and the general and ever-recurring difficulties connected with making ends meet, will all be matters of small moment to the husband in comparison with such trials as he may have to meet, and such important business claims as may come to him. Many a wife feels this under-estimation of the trials of her lot. To her, the health and happiness and education of the children, and, most of all, the making them into true, good, and holy men and women, are far from being trifling matters. On the contrary, they constitute the chief obligations of her life, and have to be attended to whatever else may befall her, while all the other host of perplexing things have to be managed by someone, or the house and its affairs will go to rack and ruin. And when the husband cannot be prevailed upon to join heart and hand with her in dealing with them, she feels it very acutely.

But what is she to do? He has no time by day. His regular hours of labor take him away the greater portion of it, and then there are other claims upon his spare time. Perhaps it is public duties or his work at the corps, or something else, that requires a large part of his leisure, and then, after retiring to rest, the wife shrinks from keeping him awake to consider such matters as the naughty lie that Johnny has told during the day, or the hacking cough of Mary in the adjoining chamber, or the rent that is coming due which she cannot see how to meet, or the serious illness of her aged mother, whom she would like to see again before she dies, or the decay of his Sunday suit, which has really become a disgrace to him—or some other of the oft-recurring trials of a home, however humble it may be.

VIII

Only too often the husband cannot afford the time even to hear about these little things, much less the spirit that boldly shares the burden. The wife has taken her full part of every anxiety that has come upon him from the first hour when they agreed to join hands and hearts together for weal or woe. But it is not thus now. A gulf is between them, and she is left to toil on with the canker at her heart, until the thousand and one anxieties worry all the religion out of her soul, worry all the true love for her husband out of her heart, and often winds up by worrying her into the grave.

Now, I say to husbands, do not let this state of things, or anything approaching to it, happen to you in your experience. Begin and go on to the end in the spirit and practice of a true partnership. The children are yours in as true a sense as they are your wife's, and although divine Providence has apportioned the larger share of the work of teaching and training them to her, a big responsibility for lending her all the assistance that lies in your power rests on you. Twenty years hence, if you are a good Salvationist, and should be spared, you will want to see them taking up a front-rank place in the battle of life, and boldly and successfully playing their part. On the other hand, you would deprecate their growing up to be the enemies of God, a curse to their fellows, and a disgrace to your name.

If the latter object is to be avoided and the former is to be gained, somebody must prepare the soil of their young hearts, put in the good seed, pull out the weeds, and watch and pray with tears and patience. I repeat again that the major portion of the burden of all this loving toil must, of necessity, fall upon the wife, and especially will it be so when the children are at the most impressionable age, but I insist also, and that with all the emphasis I can employ, that the husband must take his fair share of this anxious business—and that will largely consist in hearing about the difficulties that will be ever transpiring, counselling as to the best method of dealing with them, and encouraging the wife in the discharge of her heavenly task.

Make Your Wife Happy

8. The faithful husband will specially care for the happiness of his wife. A certain amount of gladness is essential to her health of body, mind and spirit. Men don't forget this when they think of their own lot. Their sentiment on the subject is expressed in the proverb that says, "All work and no play makes Jack a dull boy."

What is true of man, is equally true of woman. Some change of sound and scene is essential to her well-being, as much her right as his, and she ought to have it. Who is responsible for this want being supplied, if not her husband? He tried to make her happy before he married her, made her presents, and took her to meetings and festivals, shared his holidays with her at the seaside and elsewhere, spending hours conversing over matters that were unimportant in themselves and about which he cared but little, just because they made her happy for the time. Why should he not continue to use these and similar pleasing arts for making pleasant thoughts and feelings in her breast, of which he was such a master before he took her to the altar, and which will be just as acceptable and pleasing to her now as they were in the bright days gone by? I don't ask for a single one of the frivolities so common in the giddy world, but I do ask that there shall be a direct and persevering attempt to brighten her life, and make her feel that it is a joy to him to have been favored with such love as has fallen to his lot.

Alas! with many all these loving usages change so seriously, and so much for the worse as the days go by, that the poor wife comes to think that she is to her husband as an old song that has lost its charm—all the gladness dries up out of her soul, and life becomes a gloomy pilgrimage.

Of course, the experience of the true Salvationist will differ materially from this, seeing that there will be for them sources of gladness eternally new in the stream of life and salvation ever flowing in upon them, and in the ever-changing novelties connected with saving souls and extending the Kingdom of God.

How Much Time Do You Give Your Wife?

9. The true husband will give his wife a fair share of his time. This is a difficult subject, and one on which I fear some difference of opinion prevails even among Salvationists, so much so that I rather hesitate to touch it. Still, a word to the wise may be useful.

The utter selfishness of some wives is known far and near. They would ever keep their husbands dangling at their elbows, expecting them to have no higher aim than to minister to their comfort and pleasure, regardless of all the useful work they might be doing for the lost and wretched around them. But I must remark that the woman has beyond question, a right to a fair and reasonable measure of her husband's time, and he ought to see that she has it.

As Salvationists one, or both, will have ceased to live to please themselves. Their time, like all else they possess, belongs to God. To Him, and the service of His Kingdom, it has been dedicated, and the husband will have no moments to spare for giddy pleasure, either for himself or to share with his wife. But she certainly has an unquestionable claim upon her husband for the time necessary for the discharge of the duties he owes to his family. For instance, he must, if possible, find leisure for communion with God, reading the Bible and salvation literature, for teaching and training the children, and taking his part generally in the business of his own fireside. If he finds any difficulty in sparing it from other duties, let him jealously husband the moments as they fly which will alone go far to make his wife's heart glad, and his home good and happy.

IX

10. A true Salvation husband will afford his wife, so far as he is able to do so, every reasonable opportunity for exercising her gifts in Salvation work. Now, when a woman links her faith to that of her husband, she does not forego or sacrifice any of those natural rights with which she has been endowed by her Lord, and of which she finds herself possessed. No change in her earthly position, and no fresh human relationships into which she can come, can deprive her of these rights. She cannot contract herself out of them. They are her's so long as she remains

below. Look at a few of them. She has a natural right—

(a) To believe what appears to her to be the truth.

(b) To love and to obey God.

(c) To save her soul.

(d) To act as her conscience shall dictate with regard to important questions of duty.

(e) To exercise the gifts God has given her for effecting the salvation of others so far as she has opportunity for doing so, and when that exercise does not interfere with the duties she owes to her husband and her family.

No Interference

Now, no husband, at the peril of his own soul, and of bringing condemnation on the soul of his wife, must dare to ask her to sacrifice these rights, or to neglect the obligations that spring out of them. I have said before that, after her own salvation, a wife's first duties contemplate the holiness and happiness of her own home. But when, as I have shown elsewhere, the discharge of those duties can be arranged for without serious loss to anyone, she is as free to testify for Christ and to fight for souls as she was before she was married, and woe be to the husband who stands in the way of her doing so! It were better for him that a millstone were fastened round his neck, and he were cast into the midst of the sea!

But I am very sorry to say that this serious offence is very commonly committed. Are there not many women—I have known some—who have abilities that might be envied in Heaven for leading sinners to the Cross, which church arrangements or prudential family considerations, or, I fear, in some cases husbandly jealousies have consigned to silence? while, on the other hand, I have known a multitude of women whose voices, that once were heard above the clatter of the world, ringing out the message of mercy like the clarion of the Flying Angel, winning crowds to the Master's feet, are now next door to silent, or only heard now and then.

How Women Are Silenced

This closing of the mouth of woman is sometimes effected by commands directly spoken, in other cases by persuasion, while again and again I have no doubt that it comes about by petty, secret persecutions that secure the end desired by making the wife understand that her husband would prefer that she should look after her private duties—which means, very largely, that she should live for his particular gratification alone, and leave the responsibility of public effort for the salvation of souls to him.

Sometimes this silence of woman on the platform, and her retirement from public work for God, is brought to pass—and not uncommonly, I am afraid—by the loss of her own particular love for it. She marries, and is carried away by her new position, relationship and duties. They win and absorb her attention. The expulsive power of a new, or inferior, affection is proved in her case—the new, the wifely, love destroys the passion for souls enjoyed before. But more of this by and by.

11. The true husband will care for and watch over the soul of his wife. It seems as though this sentiment needed no expression. It sounds like an insult to say it to Salvationists, or any within Salvation hearing, given that they make any pretension to the membership of the great company of saints. But, alas! there are, I fear, many who, while wonderfully zealous for the sinners in the world, and the saints in their own societies neglect to deal faithfully and to guardian carefully the saints and soldiers of their own household, and, what seems the most impossible of all, they neglect the souls of their own wives. This should not be.

I have said that the wife will care for the husband's soul. I shall repeat that assertion, and have something to say upon it, when I come to talk about the duties of wives. I now want to have a word as to the husband's duty to his wife in the same direction. Is he to cherish her person, care for her temporal well-being, and find his highest satisfaction in her society for years and years, and yet all this time neglect anything like earnest, determined effort to keep her walking with God and prepared for Heaven? It seems impossible.

Who can describe the tremendous influence which a husband, who is loved and cared for gradually comes to exercise over his wife? She will go down before him almost to adoration. His will is her law, his example the pattern for her life, his opinions stand to her for infallible truth, his interests are her own, his frown is her torture, and his smile her delight, indeed, in thousands of cases, she comes to feel that Heaven would be

Hell without him, and Hell would be Heaven if he were there.

The world is full of instances of this absorption by the husband of all that is sacred in the woman's soul. If he goes right, so does she, if he goes wrong, like a lamb led to the slaughter and a sheep that before its shearers is dumb, so does she follow him. What a glorious thing when anything approaching the influence arising out of this possession by the husband if every love and passion of the woman's being is used to lead and keep her in the way of usefulness—the way that leads to Heaven! But how awful the consequences to the poor wife, and how tremendously heavy the condemnation that must rest on the husband, who exerts this influence to the diminishing of her zeal, the narrowing of her sphere of usefulness, nay, to darker consequences still—backsliding, despair and everlasting woe!

The Rattlesnake Tempter

And yet, I have known husbands, in my Army experience, who have come very near, if they have not reached, this description in all its blackness. As the rattlesnake first fascinates the innocent hummingbird and then devours its prey, so these individuals of whom we are speaking attract and ensnare the woman, in the full zenith of spiritual power and prosperity, promising all the liberty she enjoys and more. They tell her of the freedom from care they will bring her, and talk of the communion of soul that she shall enjoy, and so they win her, and, when won, the only difference between them and their victim and the rattlesnake and his comes to this—that the rattlesnake devours his victim, and they keep theirs shut up in the cage of their own home, almost, if not altogether, for the purpose of ministering to their indulgence and needs.

Oh, how many a woman might say to her husband, "Before I knew you, I was a pure, simple, believing soul. I only lived to love and serve God and to do good to man, until you came into my circle and won my affections. But you, by your secret unbelief, your zeal in public, and your indifference in private, have gone far to destroy my faith in Christian men and women, have all but made me an infidel, have all but ruined my soul!" Will any wife read these pages whose testimony of her husband's character will at all justify so terrible an indictment as that?

5

About Women and Marriage

BEFORE I GO ON to speak of the topic which naturally comes next before me, namely, the duty wives owe to their husbands, I should like to say something on the feelings with which single women ordinarily regard the question of marriage.

It is, I confess, a difficult subject for me to discuss, and would I admit, be dealt with far more effectively by a woman's pen—that is, if she were a Salvationist. But as, in this connection, the woman is not here to speak, the topic is, I think, sufficiently important to demand a word or two from me.

I
Why So Many Unmarried Women?

A large number of women must, of necessity remain unmarried, and that for two reasons:

1. There are more women in the world than men, and in some parts of it this difference is very considerable. While more males are born than females, such is the greater wear and tear of the sterner sex from wars and accidents by land and sea that men die at a faster rate than women.

2. Of the men eligible for marriage, a certain number, for various reasons—some good and some execrably bad—prefer the unmarried state.

For these reasons a certain number of women must remain single. By some this enforced spinsterhood is looked upon as a hardship, and, beyond question, to many of the sex, for a large number of reasons—to some of which I shall have occasions to refer in a succeeding paper—the state of "single blessedness," as it has been sarcastically described, is one which has produced much secret repining and no little open rebellion. To this class my sympathies not only go out, but I would fain write something that would tend to reconcile them to their lot.

Honorable Reasons For Avoiding the Marriage State

And first, I want to say that, beyond question, there is a very large number of unmarried women to whom the foregoing remarks do not in any way apply. For reasons satisfactory to themselves they have never desired marriage—indeed, in many cases, they have declined to accept opportunities for entering upon it. With others, there are family reasons—the care of beloved parents, for instance—that have deterred them from ever thinking about it.

I have known beautiful women who have been married, in spirit, to a beloved mother or an aged father, or who have had the care of the children of a deceased sister laid upon them, and who would have felt it a most serious breach of duty to abandon their trust for the marriage state. Others I have met who have been so taken up with business, or art, or literature, or the duties of some earthly position, that they have never been troubled on the question, and again, I have known many pure, beautiful women, belonging to the holy company of virgins, who have of their own choice remained single for the sake of their Master and the salvation of precious souls.

The Unmarried—But Not By Choice

Still, there are a number of unmarried women who are not so of their own free will, and who, consequently, are not happy in the station in which Providence has placed them, on the contrary, they find it difficult to believe that Providence has had much, if anything, to do with placing them there at all.

Now, with these dear comrades and sisters I want to have a word, and give a few reasons which, taken together, will go to show that marriage is not the unmixed good that youthful, and even older, imaginations are apt to put it. "It is not all gold that glitters" in the matrimonial world. With how many poor women is that fallacy destroyed before the first month has passed over their heads! How many have I known who would, after a little experience, have given their right hands to have the marriage knot untied, but mourn to find it impossible. They have made their bed, dreaming that it was to be one of roses, but wake up in anguish to find that it is an unchangeable bed of thorns!

It is quite true that, in multitudes of cases, pride or despair, or other circumstances prevent the individuals composing this sorrowing crowd from telling of the biting disappointments they suffer, and so the bitterness of their lot is endured in secret. Still, it is there. In a host of other cases, if it is not misery that follows, the change has brought with it few, if any, of the brilliant things anticipated, while it has furnished abundance of new trials, and only the family interests and instinctive love of a family make the lot endurable.

While, beyond question marriage has its advantages for both sides, it must be borne in mind that it has also its corresponding disadvantages, seen and unseen. Indeed, and specially to the woman, marriage is frequently a lottery—or, as it might fitly be termed, a leap in the dark.

Let every woman disposed to complain of being passed by, or of anticipating that she is going to be left unsought in the matrimonial sphere, look these disadvantages and risks fairly and squarely in the face, before she allows the canker-worm of discontent to eat out of her heart her confidence in her Heavenly Father's superintending care.

II

Let me submit the following for the consideration of the class to whom I am speaking:

Marriage and Health

1. No woman can be certain as to how marriage will affect her health, or whether it may not mean the sacrifice of her life. I know that marriage is said to be beneficial to the health of many women and doubtless here and there lives are prolonged by it. Indeed, I think it is said that the married live longer than the single, though that can be accounted for, I fancy, in other ways.

But whether some women are benefited physically or not, I know that a great many who have scarcely known an ache or a pain before marriage, became invalids sooner or later afterwards, and we have all known precious saints who have in childbirth been hurried home.

Heart Agreement

2. No woman can be sure how far her husband's disposition and tastes and temper will harmonize with her own sufficiently to make married life united, contented and happy. Solomon says that two cannot walk together unless they are agreed, that is, they cannot walk together harmoniously unless they are of the same opinion as to the road they should travel over, the calls they should make and a good many other particulars about the journey. But there must be an agreement between these travelers that goes deeper than these ordinary questions, if they are to journey far and long in company in peace, to say nothing about pleasure. There must be affinities between them—that is, resemblances in their characters, in their preferences, indeed, there must be an agreement in their hearts.

Now, if this agreement be necessary to comfortable companionship of two travelers who can dissolve partnership at will, how indispensable it must be to the man and the woman who will have to travel the long journey of life together, and who cannot be separated, however much they may desire it, until death do them part.

Good Individuals But Unhappy Partners

Someone has said that there are people with whom we would rather live an eternity in Heaven than a week on earth. That is on the assumption, I suppose, that these uncongenial people are going to be changed to advantage before they arrive in the world to come. Whether that be so or not, I certainly have in this life known a good many who are beyond question very good individuals, but whose society I have not cared to have longer than was absolutely necessary for the work in hand.

Are we not constantly meeting with people from whose company we are glad to get away? There is something about their spirit, their manner, their conversation that is uncongenial, that oppresses us, that jars on our nerves, and makes us glad to escape at the first convenient opportunity. What would it be, we ask sometimes, to be linked on to such people, shut in with them, as it were, for life, unable to get away, or, if we did, being compelled to come back again?

And yet that is the lot of thousands in marriage. Both parties may be excellent persons, actuated by the same holy motives in life, careful to depart from all iniquity, and follow all that is good—good officers, good soldiers, good parents—and yet so different in disposition, tastes, and temper, as to find little or no happiness in each other's society, either mental or spiritual.

Mistaken Judgments

I have no doubt it will be said in reply by the woman to whom I am writing, "Oh, I would look well and long at any man before I entered into such a lifelong union with him." That is, I suppose, what many do, and yet find, when too late, that they have been totally mistaken in the judgment they had formed, and bitterly disappointed in the expectations they had cherished, for does not the song say that "Men were deceivers ever?" I am not hinting that Salvationist comrades would willingly mislead the woman they sought for a bride, but in this respect even they naturally put on a good outside on such errands—they usually come out in their Sunday best, thus not only making the best show of themselves and their external appearance, but of their inner character when they go courting. I do not complain of it, either, for it is natural that a man should desire to stand well in every way in the eyes of the woman whom he wants to win.

Sad Infatuation

But, after all, there is no particular need for the practice of any deceptive arts, for at such times women are often so infatuated as to be oblivious to the truth, for rightly has it been said that "Love is blind." If it had not been so, how many miserable matches over which I have mourned, and labored to prevent, would never have taken place!

Oh, the instances I could give when I have striven to show female comrades the unsuitability of proposed unions on the grounds named, but labored in vain! "There are none so blind as those who will not see." In many cases I have been made to feel that the real truth is not wanted if it goes against their feelings, or, granting that the individuals may be as reported, they foolishly reckon on their ability to effect changes in character that will bring everything out right.

All I want to say is, that in marriage the woman runs considerable risks, and that in unreasonably desiring it, or lamenting that the state has been denied her, she should remember that there are a good many blanks—indeed, more blanks than prizes—and that in missing it she may have been held back from a lifetime of discomfort, if not of absolute misery.

III

3. Again, when considering the desirability of marriage, it should be remembered that no woman can be sure beforehand about her husband's secret habits. This may appear, at the first glance, to be a very similar difficulty to the one mentioned last week. But a little thought will show it is not a distinction without a difference. The former referred to natural disposition and the like, the present has to do with acquired habits. I am writing chiefly for Salvationists, and they have opportunities of discovering the truth as to a man's real character possessed, perhaps, by no other people. But how many of these have been deceived! How can a woman be quite sure that the man to whom she has entrusted her destiny—on earth at least—may not be at heart an infidel, anyway, an unbeliever, whose first work will be to instill doubts into her trusting heart, and ultimately sap the foundation of the faith she now holds dearer than life itself? How can she be quite sure he is not a secret cheat, addicted to falsehood, the slave of some lust, or in some other way the creature of habits which alone will be sufficient to destroy her happiness all the rest of her days, and to curse her children after her.

Now, I do not think, and I am not saying, that such fears ought to be sufficient to deter from marriage a woman who has prayed for guidance, and used her reason on the subject, but I am saying that the unmarried are saved from the risks I have described.

Marriage and Family Trials

4. It will be admitted at once that the woman who remains single escapes the ceaseless cares, anxieties and toils of a married life. I know, and I do not want to disguise the fact from my readers, that there are, in a large number of cases, certain joys and satisfactions to be set out against the troubles of the matrimonial state, but no one who has the opportunity of observing the toils and tears of a married woman with a family, especially if she has a small income, can deny that it often represents an

uninterrupted career of trial, stretching from the altar to the grave.

Consider the pains and perils connected with bearing and bringing a family into the world, the day and night nursing of children, the ever-recurring sicknesses that they are bound to suffer, the trials that come only too often through their waywardness in after-life. The lot of many a woman religiously married is little better than a beast of burden. She must either be shut up with the children at home, or, wandering from her prison-house, she is torn by anxieties about those she has left behind her. Added to these are a thousand other anxieties of different kinds.

I speak of it from the human standpoint. I want the single sisters to see that if they do not get all they desire in the temple of marriage, they escape much anguish by remaining outside its gates.

5. The single woman retains much freedom of action which she must forfeit, do as she will, in the marriage state. I hope to say something on the obedience a woman is bound to render to a husband in another paper, but there can be no question that marriage, to the majority of women, is little more than a respectable kind of bondage.

More Bondages

The Army has done wonders in improving the condition of married women, teaching them what their true rights really are, and disposing husbands to see that they get them. But, alas! there still remains much that is to be desired in this direction, for the natural selfishness of man, fed and fostered by the early training of foolish mothers, and the heartless notions and practices of society still regards woman as a sort of combination of servant and paramour. In some cases he adds to it the duty of ministering to his amusement, but as to making her his guide, counselor, and friend, for whose highest happiness he is constantly to seek, whose wisdom he is ever to consult, and in whose society he is to find his chief human joy, nothing could very well be further from his thoughts.

Specially does this view of things affect the condition of the Salvation Army officer. While unmarried, not only does she retain her liberty of action, being free to come and go at pleasure, regardless of the convenience of another—which is something—but she retains her freedom to work and fight for God and souls as opportunity offers. This liberty to a certain extent, she forfeits when she goes to the marriage altar.

Husbands, I am afraid, for various reasons—even Salvationist husbands—object to their wives taking too active a part in the public work. How many beautiful, devoted, and large-gifted women have I known, who, while single, swayed crowds with their divine eloquence, commanded and directed large bodies of soldiers without difficulty, and swept hundreds of souls into the Kingdom, but who comparatively speaking, passed from public view on their wedding day! They appear now and then to remind us of the treasure we have lost, and the powers that lie buried, but, so far as the free exercise of their gifts is concerned, we might almost as well have followed them to their graves as have given them over into the possession of their husbands at the marriage altar.

Now, I am not going to say that thousands of officers do not desire—nay, that they are not glad—that their beloved wives should be as fully given up to the war as ever, but there are family cares and duties that forbid. Someone must attend to them, either one or other of the couple, and the duty must be seen to fall upon the wife. Just so! And that is exactly what I am saying. The married woman not only cares to please her husband—as Paul says, "The unmarried woman careth for the things of the Lord that she may be holy both in body and in spirit, but she that is married careth for the things of the world, how she may please her husband"—but is compelled by custom and instinct to look after her children. Necessarily, therefore, she is largely shut out from the happy toil of fighting for God and winning souls.

Denied the marriage state, woman is in line with the counsels of the Apostle Paul, and is following his example.

6. Women have quite as many chances of living happy, useful, and holy single lives, as they will have married—if their opportunities are not even greater. The previous quotation from the Apostle Paul proves this. Both states have their advantages and disadvantages, and every woman may, settle it in her mind that they are about equal—nay, I should say to the Salvationist woman, who has grace to receive it, that the advantages of a single life preponderate.

7. The woman who remains unmarried for Christ's sake and the gospel's must lie very near his heart. God will, in an important sense,

be her husband, and fill up her soul with satisfaction equal to any she would reap in human marriages.

But, after all, no arguments that I can adduce will be sufficient to satisfy the ordinary run of womankind that it is good for them to abide alone. As a rule, a woman desires marriage, and that often unreasonably. At least, so it appears to me, who am able to give so many reasons for a single life after the enjoyment of so much satisfaction, reaching over so many years spent in the bonds of wedlock.

Nevertheless, and notwithstanding all that I have said—indeed, after all that anyone else can say—the marrying and giving in marriage will go forward, and in my next paper I propose to give some counsels as to the obligations under which wives are laid to their husbands.

6

The Duty of Wives to Their Husbands

WOMEN AS A RULE desire marriage, and the desire, when exercised in a reasonable degree, and in subjection to the divine pleasure, is perfectly lawful. Other and higher motives may make her quite willing to forego the realization of this desire, nay, may make it a delight for her to do so. For instance, the greater opportunity to honor her Lord and to save the souls for whom he died, may render inexpedient what would otherwise be lawful, but in the ordinary course of things, the desire for the married state is as proper in woman as it is in man, and that amongst others for the following reasons:

I
Man and Woman Created for Each Other

1. Marriage is the gratification of a natural instinct. If man was not created for the woman, then woman was created for the man and is not complete without him. He is, so to speak, a part of her, and the two parts are necessary to the making of one complete whole, indeed, until they are brought together there will be a measure of unrest and disquietude on the part of both.

2. Marriage meets the yearning of the woman's soul for a closer human communion than she can ordinarily find elsewhere. Woman's nature is pre-eminently sympathetic. She was made for friendship. She wants some other heart to rest in. Man can get on better alone than woman, seeing that he has so many other aims, recreations, ambitions, and the like to occupy him. Woman, so differently circumstanced, has her whole fortune in her affections, wants a kindred soul on whom she can lavish them, and a husband seems to be the natural object for her love.

It is true that there have been, and are, any number of beautiful instances of this fellowship of spirit existing between woman and woman.

There are many in the Army, as we observed in our last paper, who pour out all their store of love after this fashion, or place it in some sacred and beautiful sacrifice, directly at the Master's feet. But with others it is not so. They ask for the fellowship of marriage, and are only able to find that satisfaction there.

3. The woman desires marriage because of the material—the earthly—advantages it offers. Perhaps she is poor, and has no one to provide for her. Perhaps she is weak and has no one to defend her. Perhaps she is lonely, and has no one to companion her, and she reasons, "Who can supply these needs so well as a husband?" It is felt by woman no less than by man, that it was intended he should be the means of provision and defence to the weaker sex, therefore, what so natural that she should seek to link her fate with his? He is constituted her natural guardian.

It may be said that this reason is an unworthy one. I do not think so. Is the woman not prepared to give to man, in her love, and sympathy, and service, a fair exchange for all he gives to her? The man who finds a wife, the inspired prophet says, finds "a good thing." We might truthfully add to it "a good bargain." In fact, he may be said to have made his fortune.

Some Women Kept in Bondage

But the very semblance of unworthiness is removed by a moment's consideration of the unnatural conditions into which society has brought woman. "It is true that great changes have been wrought of late in many communities, but until the other day what employments were there open to a woman by which she could earn her daily bread, except those of the most menial character, indeed, little better, in many cases, than slavery? And even now things are not very much better, so that a woman is driven to choose between domestic service, factory work, and other similar forms of toil—for which she know she will only be acceptable in early life—and that of matrimony. No wonder that she should prefer the latter!

Then again, is she not trained in her childhood in the belief that she must marry or be an everlasting drudge? Do not her mother, and her father, and her brothers and sisters, and relations, and all about her, din it into her ears continually that marriage is her destiny, and that if she misses it her life is a failure, so far as this world goes?

It is true that this state of things does not exist in the Salvation Army, where new opportunities of service have been opened for her. But there is a great deal of it even there. Still, these employments are only possible to a section of the thousands of the precious women who march under the yellow, red and blue. But even in the Army, woman looks forward to marriage as the best way of finding a comfortable home, and the provision for her need in this life, and no one can justly condemn her for doing so.

An Important Instinct Explained

4. The maternal instinct leads women to desire marriage. To ensure the propagation of the race, God has planted certain desires, or appetites in the physical system, which are essential to the continuance of the race, and the gratification of which, after the plan intended by God, is as lawful as that of any other physical appetite. But for the natural craving for food, men would not be at the trouble to seek it, and the race would become extinct, and but for the desire referred to, such would be the disinclination of woman to face the pains and toils connected with family life, that no more children would be born into the world, and man would die out from the face of the earth.

This maternal instinct is strong in most women. The sacred gift of motherhood, that wonderful passion which carries her without flinching or complaint through years of service and sacrifice for her children, awakes early, and before all earthly things she desires to become the mother of a living child. Marriage is the only legitimate and honorable way by which that craving can be fulfilled, and hence her desire to enter into that state.

When the marriage has taken place, then the rule before referred to in the case of the husband must be taken as applying equally to the wife, namely, that the advantages conferred by marriage upon the wife impose certain obligations in return.

II

1. The wife is under obligation to obey. If the husband, in character and conduct, is all that he should be, if he reaches the ideal—that is, the

standard I have set for him in a previous chapter—then the obedience required from, and rendered by, his wife will be little more than a name. In fact, there will be as much obedience on the one side as on the other. This was largely, if not absolutely, the case in the union between my precious wife and myself. There was no feeling of firstness or mastery with either the one or the other, and all sense of obedience was lost in the desire to mutually meet each other's wishes.

2. Indeed, where there is a strong affection on the part of the wife, there will be little difficulty on this question. The danger will ordinarily be in the opposite direction, namely, that of going over to the extreme of obedience. The woman will be likely to subordinate her judgment—her object in life—her sense of duty to both God and man—to her husband, and, under the influence of her affection and admiration for him, go down and become his creature—I might say his willing slave. How often we see this in the case of women every way stronger than their husbands in all those points of character most valuable and useful, and, indeed, in those graces also that are most precious of all!

Obedience the General Rule for Woman

3. But it will be wise for women to always bargain in their own minds for obedience, whether it becomes the pleasure I have described or not. They will, as a rule, reap more liberty of action by doing so than by any resolutions or attempts at standing up for what they may deem their rights. The woman who is determined to have her own way in opposition to her husband's judgment, and be her own mistress ought not to marry at all. Let the latter class beware of promises made before marriage. Husbands will promise many things before the event, and that with the intention of fulfilling them, but, when the time comes round, will fail in their pledges, not of set purposes, but because the circumstances will be too strong for them. No, one way or the other, there is nothing for it but for the wife to make up her mind to the possibility of being subject all the rest of her days to the will of her husband, and that in things that are nearest and dearest to her.

4. She is under obligation to love and cherish her husband, before all else beside. She must have no human love before him, that is, no female friend or relative, inside or outside her house.

Of course, I am supposing that the husband gives to the wife the love and the communion that are due her. Should he, however, fail in this—if he carries his confidences and companionships away from home—he can hardly complain if his poor, lonely wife does the same. But the rule is, the husband first.

5. The wife is under obligation to care for the health, and home, and all that concerns the physical interests of her husband. In some way or other, whether from instinct or custom or something else, it is felt to be the wife's duty to take the responsibility for the keeping of his house, the preparation of his food, the supervision of his clothing, together with a general care for his health. To these a wife must give her attention, and for these she must hold herself responsible.

Fidelity

6. I need not say that the wife is under obligation to keep herself to her husband alone. Infidelity is terrible when it occurs in the husband, and, in the eyes of Divine Justice, as sinful as in the wife—doubtless in many cases it is much more so. But, after all, a higher standard of purity and rectitude in all that concerns the sexual relations has been, by mutual consent, set up for the woman. If she falls, it is from a loftier height, and, therefore, she descends to a lower depth of infamy and woe. Tempted many wives doubtless are, and while the world is full of fiendish, lustful men, tempted she will be, but she must walk the narrowest path of purity, keeping her inmost thoughts and feelings faithful to her husband.

7. Neither need I say that the wife is under the most sacred obligations to love, cherish, and seek the highest interests of her husband's children. This duty may, and will involve her, as we have had occasion again and again to observe, in a life of anxiety, self-sacrifice and care. But there is no alternative. They are there. They belong to her in even a higher and tenderer sense than they do to him. She must watch over and protect them and seek to supply their every need for time and for eternity.

8. And lastly, I would remark that the wife is under obligation to care for her husband's soul, and aim at his everlasting salvation. This is the most solemn and binding obligation of all, and yet, I am afraid,

it is one not uncommonly neglected.

"Oh," said the wife of a husband who had gone sadly astray the other day. "I have cared for his health, nursed his children, looked after his earthly comforts, but I have forgotten his soul."

7

About the Duties Parents Owe to Their Children and The Training Required

Solemn Obligations

THE POSSESSION OF THESE advantages must impose upon parents solemn obligations for doing all that in them lies to promote the highest welfare of their children. How far that obligation extends! "How shall we order the child, and how shall we do unto him?" was the inquiry made by the father of Samson when informed of his coming birth. It seems perfectly natural to me that all parents should make a similar inquiry with respect to the children God may entrust to their keeping. Before any satisfactory answer can be given to the question, another inquiry must be replied to, that is: "What do you want to make the child into? What is the future you desire for it?"

Let me look at the child from that standpoint. What is, or what ought to be, the ambition of the Salvationist parents for their children? I need not say that they will desire something higher and nobler than to make the child a mere plaything, a kind of doll for them to fondle, and dress up, and get amusement out of. That would, indeed, be a low level on which to place the treasure which God has committed to their charge.

Neither need I say that they will picture and aim at a nobler future for the child than its merely becoming their drudge.

Neither will they be content to train and shape it for becoming a creature of the world, satisfied with its riches, pleasures, and recreations, while living in rebellion against God, and joining hands with the multitudes traveling to destruction.

No! The true Salvationist has a very different object to anything like the foregoing before his eyes. He will want:

I
The Salvationist's Aim

1. To make his children good—that is, truthful, honest, industrious, kind, fit for the companionship of the righteous on earth, and for the presence of God and the angels in Heaven.

2. To bring his children into the family of God, which means being converted, receiving a new heart, and being so endued by the Holy Spirit, as to be able to walk in holiness and truth in whatever station in life they may come to occupy.

3. To make them soldiers in the Army, to inspire them, while young, with a passion for the fight, making them love the soul-saving work, and delight in the prospect of being officers in the Army, or filling whatever post they may be found equal to, expecting to follow Christ, bearing his cross, enduring tribulation, and doing his will.

That is the aim of the Salvationist, whether officer or soldier, with other people's children, both young and old. Nothing less ought to satisfy him for his own. I need not stay a moment to impress upon the minds of my readers the nobility and utility of the object I have so hurriedly sketched out for them. It will, I feel certain, strike deep into the hearts of the fathers and mothers who will read it over, and every one of them will desire to see it realized in their dear children. How this is to be done, I propose to show in the chapter that follows.

How Not to Do It

I need not occupy any time in setting forth the self-evident truth that a certain course of training will be necessary if the average run of children are to come up to the standard described in the previous chapter. However desirable it may appear to parents that their children should be good and godly, and grow up to be holy men and women, and however much they may pray for such a blessed result, unless they use the means to bring it about they will never have the joy of its realization. The children must be trained, and I want to describe the sort of training that will be likely to secure the result. In doing so, it has occurred to me that it will be useful to commence by protesting against some of the kinds of treatment children not uncommonly receive, which are not likely to succeed and begging my comrades not to imitate them.

Don't! Don't!! Don't!!!

1. Don't set the things that are earthly and temporal, at any time or in any fashion, before the things that are heavenly and eternal, and then complain that your children grow up to prefer the world and its charms to following Christ in holiness and sacrifice for the salvation of men. That is, don't do things in your home, or anywhere else in the presence of your children, that will make the impression on them that making money, pleasing people, gratifying themselves, or any other worldly things, are of greater moment than pleasing God, keeping a good conscience, or saving souls, without expecting that they will grow up to act on the same principle, and after the same fashion, only in a fuller degree.

2. Don't act as though you believed and expected that human nature, left to itself, will develop into the godly, holy, self-sacrificing character that you desire, and then be disappointed if your children turn out little devils, or grow up to be big ones, instead of becoming angels of light. That is, don't expect a clean thing to come out of an unclean. And if your children are not born with evil natures, as some teach—and as there is much in the Scriptures and our own observations to justify—they certainly become possessed of selfish and naughty hearts very early. Anyone who observes children can see that by the time they reach the age of reason and know right from wrong, they are the bond-slaves of their appetites, which ever lead them astray, so that, unless the grace of God changes their hearts and makes them new creatures, they will be certain to grow up, if not actually vicious, yet proud, worldly, selfish, and devilish, like the world around them.

II

3. Don't expect that children who have any natural force of character, any backbone in them, and who, therefore, are worth saving, will be likely to submit their wills, first to their parents and then to God, without a great deal of patient and persevering effort.

There will be exceptions. No doubt there are many children who, though they find little natural opposition to the things of God in the stubbornness of their own natures, are, nevertheless, strong characters, and make glorious saints. Samuel seems to have been one such. I have some in my own family. But we do not know what secret conflicts they may have had before the inward opposition ceased, and they were able to say, "Thy will be done." Be that as it may, if you want your children, and the strongest of your children, for the King, you must in no case be deterred from persevering until you conquer.

Be Real

4. Don't expect your children to be such simpletons as not to be able to see beneath the cloak of sham religion, and, having discovered its unreality, heartily despise it. Don't be suspicious if, in after life, they should make such hypocrisy an excuse, secretly or publicly, for utterly neglecting, if not positively disbelieving, religion.

5. Don't expect your children to be any better in their conduct and character, than the example set before them in their early days, in their own home, and by their own kindred and friends. Allow your children to associate with half-hearted professors, worldly pharisees, or backslidden saints generally, whether soldiers or otherwise, and you must not be surprised if they are cursed by their example, and perhaps driven from true religion altogether.

Children will be likely to get more harm by staying in the house of a Laodicean, or a make-believe follower of Christ, than by staying a month in a drinking saloon, where they know the devil reigns and his works prevail.

Keep Clear of Finery

6. Don't pervert the natural love of the beautiful, which will doubtless be born in the hearts of some of your children, into vanity, by creating a taste for fine clothes, jewelry, and the like, or by filling them with the childish conceit that they have prettier faces, figures, hair, or some other physical advantage, than those about them, and then wonder that they should in after years be dragged into the world, and down to Hell, through the love of its fashions and follies.

Don't fill your children up with notions of their own superiority, whether mentally or in any other way, and so send them out into life the slaves of the desire to excel their fellows.

Give Girls Their Right Place

7. Don't create, or even allow, the notion in your boys that they are of more value in the world, or more important, than the girls, and then be surprised that they should domineer over them, or grow up to treat a wife, or woman generally, as if she belonged to an inferior race—which she does not.

8. Don't coddle your children, and make them spoony, or humor and spoil them until they are a nuisance to themselves and everybody about them unless they are everlastingly being waited upon, amused, or allowed to have their own way.

9. Don't foster the natural selfishness of your children. We have seen that they are carried away by the desire for self-gratification at the onset of their earthly career. Your business is to drive them in the opposite direction, to make them seek to deny themselves, and to delight to work for other people.

10. Don't instill, or allow anybody else to instill, into the hearts of your girls the idea that marriage is the chief end of life. If you do, you must not be surprised if they get engaged to the first empty, useless fellow they come across.

III
How Not To Do It

11. Don't argue or discuss matters that concern the conduct or character of children, about which there is any difference between you, in their presence, and then be surprised if they take sides with the one or the other whose notions they most favor.

12. Don't have any favorites amongst your children, and then be surprised that the remainder should grow up with a sense of injustice rankling in their breasts, the memory of which will be in danger of making them forget all the love and sacrifice you have endured for them in the past.

13. Don't let your children have their own way, or give them things they want, when doing so is opposed to your own judgment, merely for the sake of peace, and then be surprised if they argue and contradict you,

and finally come to ridicule your wishes and opinions before the family, if not to set you at naught ever after.

14. Don't wink at disobedience and other acts of wrong-doing in your children, when you happen to be particularly occupied, or to have company, or to be in an amused state of mind, and then burst out into condemnation or punishment when you happen to be tired or irritated about other things. Don't act thus if you don't want them to think that you are weak, or that you don't know your own mind, or that your dealings with them are governed by your feelings at the hour either of which notions will be sufficient to sap their confidence in your justice, and therefore fatal to your power over them.

15. Don't expect God to save your children, and carry them up to a good, wise and useful manhood and womanhood, without your doing for them those things on which these blessed results are made to depend. Parents don't expect salvation for themselves or their neighbors without the fulfillment of the conditions laid down in the Bible. God has conditioned the salvation of the children on the performance of certain duties by the parents. Why should they expect God to save their children on any other terms? If they do, they will very likely be disappointed.

Some Things Parents Must Do

I closed my last section by remarking that there are some things that parents must not do if they are to make their children into saints and soldiers. To attain this very desirable result, doubtless may, and will, be a very difficult undertaking, costing you much anxiety and toil, but there is little that is truly good or great accomplished in this world without these qualities, and whatever measure of them this work may call for, if you succeed it will be found to be well worth the outlay—you will be abundantly repaid. What the things are that you must do, I want to point out. In the compass of these short chapters, however, I can do little more than name them:

(1) You must keep the object you have in view for you children constantly before your mind. I have already set it forth, you know it well. Look it well in the face, and resolutely determine to accomplish it. Do not let any of the blandishments of the world, or the temptations of the devil, or the promptings of your own ease and pleasure, turn you aside.

Oh fathers and mothers, you must do or die!

(2) You must believe in the possibility of success. What you desire can be done—has been done, and what parents have done, parents can do again. Do not be deterred by the failure of others—though they are sadly too plentiful in every direction. Say to yourself, in the face of all breakdowns, "If the children of Parson Flashem, Deacon Swellum, Bishop Creedum, and Captain Weedum, have not turned out well, nay, if some of them have gone to the bad altogether, that is no rule for me. There has been something wrong in the training, or the example, or the schooling, or something. God's Word says, 'Train up a child in the way he should go, and when he is old he will not depart from it.' I am going to do the training as well as I can, and God must see to the success of it." Have faith in God, my friends, and he will come to your assistance.

> *Ask the Savior to help you,*
> *Strengthen, comfort and bless you,*
> *He is willing to aid you,*
> *He will carry you through.*

3. Create and confirm in the hearts of your children the belief that you are yourselves what you wish them to become. Without this, you will be a dead failure and a stumbling-block. You must present, in your daily life, the example of unselfish love and righteousness which you ask from them.

4. Instruct your children as to what true religion really is. Make them understand as soon as they can understand. Base your preaching on the precepts and examples given in the Bible, especially on the life and death of the Lord Jesus Christ.

5. Make them feel the rightness of all that you ask for them. Appeal to their judgment and conscience rether than to their feeligs, although you cannot do without the latter. But you must make them understand. Come down to the level of their capacity and intelliegence--that is, of what they already know. There is a difference between being simple and being silly. People who talk to children do not often observe the distinction. But *you* must! Make them understand what you do teach them. Use singing, and pictures, anecdotes, lones upon line, here a little and there a

little, and you will succeed.

6. Insist upon perfect obedience to all your commands; indeed, to all your expressed wishes. You must have this obedience or all your other efforts will be practically thrown away. It is impossible to over-estimate the importance of the formation of the habit of obedience. It enters into every other duty. Prepare the hearts of your children for the xercise of the rightful affection to parents, and the entrance on the service of God. In fact, the infant complying willingly with the wish of its mother is rendering true worship to God.

Settle it in your soul, therefore, from the first vision of your babe, and the first kiss you impress upon its cheek, that, before all else, you have to inculcate the habit of obedience into its young soul. How is this to be done? I want to show:

1. Begin early. It is astonishing how soon the infant in its mother's arms can be taught that it must do her will, and not its own.

2. Do not give too many commands to young children. But what are given, you must be at the trouble to have obeyed. How often you will hear fathers and mothers call upon their children to do this, or that, or the other, without waiting, or even caring, to see whether they do either. What can be the result of such treatment in the minds of the children, but that it does not matter whether they obey at all? Never ask a child to do a thing, or to leave a thing undone, without insisting on obedience.

3. Be careful that your commands are within the ability of your children. It is cruel to ask children to do what is outside their power, and yet I am afraid that parents are thoughtlessly addicted to the practice. While they would never dream of requiring them to carry burden for which they had not sufficient strength, or read in a language they had not learned, they will insist on the little child sitting motionless and silent, and not crying when it has a pain, or going to sleep when it is too excited from fright or other causes—all of which are just as far beyond the ability of the child, if not as absolutely impossible. Be tender and considerate in the commands you give to your children.

4. Be careful that your orders are good and lawful; otherwise, how can you insist on obedience?

5. Be careful that your commands are understood. Some people have a hurried manner of speaking, or they are not at the trouble to explain the

duty; hence the children, not comprehending what is asked of them, are unable to comply with the request.

Now, when you ask for something to be done, not only be at the trouble to make the duty plain, but close up your instruction by asking the question: "Do you understand what it is that I want you to do?" Specially should this be the case when there appears to be any hesitancy about complying with the command.

6. When the task you desire from your children appears extra difficult, or you have any idea that it is particularly uncongenial to them, be at a little trouble beforehand to show its reasonableness, and that it will be an advantage to the child, or to the family, or to someone else. Also set forth the pleasure it will give you, if it is done properly and well.

7. Be sure to mark your disapproval of disobedience by some appropriate punishment. This is a necessity. You cannot pass known disobedience by without notice. To do so would be to adopt one of the surest methods of cursing your child for the present and the future. Nothing stands out more prominently in the divine government than the connection of punishment with sin. It must be so in your government of your children. You stand in the place of God to them. Disobedience is not only a sin, but it lies at the foundation of all other sins. You are bound by your faithfulness to God. You live for His glory, and your concern for the maintenance of righteousness in your household will lead you to inflict some penalty on the wrong-doer.

8. You must inflict the necessary punishment. It is very impossible that you will be favored with children so good and truthful and obedient as never to need punishment, therefore it is important that you should have correct notions on this subject. And my first counsel is:

1. Before punishing, be sure that the child is guilty of the offence brought against it. Nothing can be much more painful to the parent, or injurious to the child, than the infliction of punishment that is not deserved. Be sure, also, that the offense was intelligently and deliberately committed. If the child did not know that it was doing wrong, and did not intend to do the deed, then there is no wrong to punish.

2. While punishment is deserved, let it be prompt. The sooner it follows the act of wrong-doing, the more effective it will be.

3. While punishment is sharp, so that it will be remembered, it should

be of as short duration as is consistent with the gravity of the offence. This in favor of the rod. A little whipping will be remembered, and yet, being soon over, will not unnecessarily prolong any torture.

4. Care should be taken that neither corporal nor other punishment be injurious to health. It is quite possible to damage a child's nervous system for a life-time by the infliction of too severe or too protracted pain, either by flogging, solitary confinement or other penalties. However naughty, disobedient, or cruel children may have been, justice must be tempered with mercy.

5. The punishment inflicted must be as nearly as possible, the best adapted to secure repentance. Two ends should be before every parent in discharging the duty;

(a.) The infliction of punishment for its own sake. Suffering and wrong-doing are already closely associated in the heart of the child. When he does a wrong thing his own instincts tell him that he ought to suffer for it. You should strengthen that conviction, so that in after life, if he is spared, he shall feel that if he lives and dies in sin, Hell will be righteous portion.

(b.) When you punish a child, your aim should be to bring him to repentance thereby. You want him to see and feel how naughty he has been, how wrong it all was, what misery naughtiness makes, and to bring him to the resolution that he will do so no more.

(c.) In punishing children parents should be careful to inflict no more suffering than is calculated to attain the object in view. To do so would be unjust—nay, absolutely cruel. A mother's or father's heart will prevent the infliction of such a wrong.

IV
No Long Fights

6. In inflicting punishment avoid, as far as possible, anything like protracted conflicts with your children. From some strange motive, or from no intelligible motive at all, there will occasionally be a blank refusal on the part of a child to obey some distinct command. Now, at such times, the course ordinarily adopted by parents will be to compel obedience at all costs, and it is no uncommon experience for there to be a regular battle between the parties.

The parent says, "My boy refuses to pronounce a word in his lessons, or to close a door, or to do something else that I have commanded him. The act itself is a trivial matter, but the obedience is of lasting importance. I must compel that obedience at all hazards."

The boy, in some strange and infatuated spirit, obstinately refuses. Punishment follows, the boy still refuses. Then come alternate pleadings, scoldings, weepings and prayers—all of which the boy meets with the same dogged refusal, and so the conflict will be carried on for hours, to the heart-breaking distress of the parents and the unutterable wretchedness of the child. At length, the boy surrenders, and the parent feels a measure of satisfaction in having secured the obedience which he feels to be of lifelong advantage to the child.

Try Bed Before Cane

Now, there can be no question about the importance of securing the repentance and submission of the boy. But is the plan which I have described the best? I submit that it is not. I would advise that instead of entering on this discussion, the child be sent to bed on the first act of disobedience, prayed with, the character of his disobedience being explained to him, and so left to his own reflections. The probability is that on the following morning he will volunteer a confession of his fault, and promise that it shall never occur again. If he does not follow this course, then, as with other evil-doings, he must be placed out of the bounds of your pleasure until he does.

7. You must make religion an affair of your everyday life. The children must feel that you are as religious at home as in the barracks, on Mondays as on Sundays, in your work as on your knees, indeed, it should be the atmosphere of the house, so that in it they can live and breathe, move and have their being.

Get Them Converted

8. Aim at a distinct experience of conversion in your children. There is a line that divides the righteous from the wicked. There is a moment when human beings, adults or children, cease to be the servants of the devil, and become the children of God. That line, and that moment, may be approached so gradually as to be crossed all but imperceptibly, the

experience of the moment not differing so remarkably from that which has gone before it as to make any marked impression on the soul. But with God's own servants and soldiers the line is crossed, and the moment is experienced, when their hearts are regenerated and their characters changed, when they pass from darkness to light, from death to life, from being under the power of Satan to being under the power, protection and blessing of God. In other words, they are saved.

Now, you must aim at that distinct experience for your children. You must explain to them its nature and necessity. You must pray for it separately and together. You must lead them to expect it at the meetings or alone, and you will have the high privilege of knowing that it has taken place, and of hearing them testify to the fact.

Make Them Strong

9. You must do all that in you lies to promote their bodily health. Whether they shall be feeble, nervous creatures, or strong and vigorous as men and women, depends very much upon your treatment of them in childhood.

What a mercy it is for Salvation fathers and mothers that the plainest and cheapest foods, and the simplest clothes, should be the best! That fresh air, and exercise, and sleep should cost nothing! That soap and water should be within reach of all, or nearly all, and that all these things, taken together, should be calculated to make strong and healthy bodies!

Let Their Education Be Simple

10. You must do all you can for the minds of your children. You want to make them wise and thoughtful. They will be men and women soon. You won't want to be the parents of fools and failures, but of wise men and women. Act accordingly. However poor and humble you may be, simple education is within your reach. See that your children get it.

Interest yourself in what your children learn. Find out whether they are doing their best. Stimulate and encourage, and, if you can, assist them.

11. Do what you can to make your children truthful, honest, honorable and generous.

12. Strive to make your children industrious. I have already said encourage them to work at their lessons. Give them some work apart from their books that they can perceive is of some real value.

13. Make your children juniors. Encourage them to look forward to being corps cadets. Regularly see the Junior sergeant, and inquire as to their conduct at the company meetings, and as to the progress they are making.

14. Rely on the Holy Spirit to bless all your efforts. He will rejoice to help you, for is not the promise of salvation alike to you and your children?

Fathers, Take Note

15. Both parents must unite in these duties. They will not both do the same thing, but father must do his share, and mother must do hers, and one must strengthen the other. It is not uncommon, I am afraid, for many fathers to leave the weight of the obligation, especially in childhood, on the mother. This is not right.

16. You must persevere. Perhaps no task undertaken by the people of God calls for more patience and endurance than that of making children into saints and soldiers of Jesus Christ, and perhaps, no reward can compare, in satisfaction and gladness, with that which comes to the mothers and fathers who succeed.

8

The Black Sheep

IN MANY, IF NOT in the majority of flocks, if they be of any reasonable size, there will be a wanderer from the fold, who may truthfully be styled the black sheep of the family. It may be the son, the daughter, or alas! one of the parents, or it may be some member of the household who, from association or other reasons, is as precious even as those who stand in that relationship I have named.

It does not follow that this wanderer shall have gone openly or flagrantly into the ways of sin and vice, or that they should have wandered off into a far country—that is, that they should have become drunkards, or gamblers, or the like, or that they should have fled from home. No, they may be moral in outward character and conduct, still residents under the same old roof, and yet be separate in spirit, belief, and action from those views and feelings which are dearest to the hearts of the loved ones around.

This is a painful, nay, a heart-breaking, experience. The peace and gladness of any number of fathers and mothers have been destroyed by it, while their health has been broken, and their feet turned into the way that leads to an early grave. Love is a wonderful thing. It often thrives on the very food, the very diet, which you would have imagined would have annihilated it. Day and night the form of the wrongdoer is present with those most sinned against, and day and night the prayer ascends to Heaven for his salvation. What is to be done, it may be asked, under such circumstances?

I
Things That Won't Help You

1. Needless self-reproach will not help you. Amongst Salvationists, as well as others outside our borders, parents may have to deal with the

bitter reflection that perhaps their own former sinful life may have influenced their children for evil. It may be so, or perhaps the want of that direct, and definite training for a holy life, for which they are responsible, may have helped to cause this melancholy result But even in that case, it cannot be helped now. You cannot go back to those days and live them over again. If you could, you would, but you cannot, and God has forgiven your sins and your neglect. They are gone, and nothing will be gained by moaning and wailing about the matter.

2. Unreasonable condemnation of the wrongdoer will not help you. They are sinners, doubtless great sinners, but are we not all sinners? And, probably, something can be said in their favor. They were strongly tempted, they went down, perhaps, by steps, they never intended to reach the depths to which they have sunk, they are ashamed of it themselves—if ever they dare to reflect upon it. There will be condemnation, strong condemnation, but it must be accompanied by compassion, by an abundance of pity, for condemnation alone will not help you—it will only sour your own spirit, and interfere with your own peace.

3. Neither will the condemnation of those who led your prodigal astray help you. You will not be able to avoid feeling deeply the wrong that has been done to you and yours, and yet your sense of injury must be tempered with mercy. You have to follow the example of your Lord, and pray for your enemies.

II

Then, what is to be done with this dark and heavy trial? I reply: You must use such means as lie within your ability, and that are likely to secure the salvation of the wanderer.

Measures That Will Succeed

1. I need not say that you must pray. That is old-fashioned advice, but no worse for that. It is counsel which anyone can give you, and which anyone who has any knowledge but there is nothing better. You must pray. Prayer will bring you into communion with God, and he will comfort your heart. In sorrow, who is so able to cheer you as those who have suffered after the same fashion? Jesus Christ has had, and still has, many black sheep in his flock. He had when he was on earth, he has today. He

suffered in order to be able to understand and sympathize with his suffering people when brought into similar conditions.

Prayer will keep your own spirit bright, nay, prayer will sanctify the misfortune to your benefit, and so make it work together for your good. Prayer will bring God to your help. He will answer if he can. Up to a certain level you can be quite sure that he will give you the thing for which you ask. He will trouble the conscience, create the desire to return, open the way for the prodigal to do so, and if the lost sheep does not return from the wilderness, you can be quite sure that only determined, willful obstinacy on his part is the hindrance.

Personal Pleading

2. Appeal personally. Plead with the wanderer yourself. It should be done wisely, but, wherever possible, it should be done. One of the most painful devices to which wrong-doers of this class revert, is the attempt at self-justification. By false accusation of others, they will say to those whose hearts they have broken, "Perhaps I am wrong, but is it not your fault? Did you not govern me with too tight a hand? or did you not allow false accusation to be brought against me? or did you not deny me the enjoyment of reasonable privileges? You have only your own self to thank for what has happened." And so insult and falsehood are added to the injury already inflicted.

In the whole course of human suffering I know of nothing more painful to endure than this. This sort of thing makes personal dealing not only difficult, but often an agony. Still, it is a duty, and must be discharged. If the desired result is not gained at the moment, it may help in the future, and if it does not bring restoration and salvation to the wanderer then, or afterwards, it will bring strength to your own heart for the endurance of the trial, and when you lie on the banks of the river, and look over the past, the consciousness of having done what in you lay for your sinning loved one, will help your peace and afford you satisfaction.

Letters and Messages

3. If you cannot appeal personally with your own words and tears, you can write. What if your letters are consigned to the fire, and torn in pieces, and scattered to the winds, or returned to you unread, or

even refused acceptance? That is not your business. Your work is to appeal, to explain, to entreat. The responsibility for results must rest on other shoulders.

4. You can send messengers who will represent your feelings. There are Salvation Army officers scattered up and down the world who will be glad to be your servants, for Christ's sake, in this matter. Interest them in your strayed sheep, get them to intercede for you. If you can afford it, pay their traveling expenses. Tell them to say that you have sent them—that you are longing after them—praying for them—waiting for their return—willing to forgive and forget all if they will only repent, and cast themselves on the mercy of God. Thousands and thousands have been won after this fashion, and your wanderer may prove no exception.

Strong Faith

5. Have faith in God. Means are excellent, they are necessary. Letters and appeals, private and public, are in the order of God's arrangement. He has decreed that they should be used. There will be little or no success without them, but with all, and above all, you must have faith in God. You must keep him in your business. If you attempt to carry your cause and gain your point without reference to him, you will fall. He will not be left out. It is God who saves, and in order that you may keep him interested and active in all your thinkings, feelings, weepings, prayings, appealings, and everything else, you must rely on him for cooperation and success.

6. Above and beyond all, you must never give up. While there is life, there is room and ground for hope. "While the lamp holds out to burn, the vilest sinner may return." The world is full of wonderful instances in which the patient perseverance of mother and father in seeking their lost sons and daughters have been rewarded with success.

—Part Two—
The Soul

9

About Being Saved—The Forgiveness of Sin

WHAT A WONDERFUL THEME this salvation is of which I am writing to you! I feel it so. My own heart is full of wonder and astonishment at the wisdom and mercy of God as I write. Indeed, the more I contemplate it the more I feel it is impossible to tell you half the glory and blessedness of his grace. I remember some curious lines, in which an old poet describes the love of God, and what he says of that love might with equal truth be written of this great salvation.

> Could I with ink the ocean fill,
>   Were every blade of grass a quill,
> Were the whole sky of parchment made,
>   And every man a scribe by trade,
> To write the love of God on high
>   Would drain that ocean dry—
> Nor could the scroll contain the whole,
>   Though stretched from sky to sky.

I

The first blessing is "The Forgiveness of Sins," and can anything be more important or interesting? Let us look at it thoughtfully.

And first I must ask what we are to understand by sin? Upon that subject there seem to be many mistaken notions abroad. Some think that to sin you must be guilty of some vulgar or shameful vice. They seem to imagine that it does not matter how you treat God if you don't deny his existence or blaspheme his holy name. That it does not matter how you treat your neighbor if you do not rob him of his property or damage his person. That it does not matter how you treat yourself if you don't actually lay hands on your own life.

By this, I mean that many people seem to think that God won't call them to account for these small evils, as they call them, if they stop short of the blacker and more avowed transgressions of laws both human and divine. You can be proud and selfish and revengeful and idle and untruthful and insincere, and I know not what, and in their idea it need not interfere with your respectability before men or your acceptance with God. But if you are a murderer, or a thief, or an adulterer, or a drunkard, then they will put you down as an awful sinner, deserving of the terrible judgments of God, both here and hereafter, and say that "you should go to the Salvation Army."

Now, I need not tell you how grossly false these notions are. You know it already, as well as I know it myself. "What a man thinketh in his heart that is he."

But I will try to make the truth about sin plainer still, by asking information from those who understand the question a long way better than I do myself. Of whom shall we inquire? We will ask the Apostle John. He understood the matter.

"John, will you please tell us what is sin?" Now listen to his answer. John says in his first letter, which is largely filled up with this subject, and which you will do well to carefully read over and over again, "Sin is the transgression of the law."

"But of what law?" Jesus Christ himself has answered that question. When the lawyer asked him, "Which is the great commandment?" The Savior replied, "Thou shalt love the Lord thy God with all thy heart, and with all thy soul, and with all thy mind. This is the first and great commandment. And the second is like unto it, Thou shalt love thy neighbor as thyself. On these two commandments hang all the law and the prophets." So that is the law, and we are under obligation to keep it; it is the law of love.

Is not that a beautiful arrangement? Sometimes you will hear people say, "We don't like being driven to duty by the hope of reward or the fear of punishment. Don't talk to us," they will say, "about death and judgment or hell as incentives to religion. We like to do things from a sense of duty, prompted only by the spirit of love."

That is just God's plan, my comrades, both for you and for me. He wills that we should keep his commandments because we love him. He wills that we should follow Jesus Christ because we love him. He wills that we should do all the good we can to our comrades and neighbors because we love them. He wills that we should toil and fight for poor sinners because we love them. That is God's plan, or law, as it is called. I say again, that when men don't act out God's plan they go contrary to the law of love, and then they sin.

But John has another explanation of sin that appears to be simpler still. He says, "All unrighteousness is sin," but I cannot dwell on it, and besides it really needs little explanation. By unrighteousness God means anything that is not right, that is, anything that is wrong. So that whatever course of conduct God, by his Word or Spirit, or by his servants, or by your own conscience, makes you see and feel to be wrong, to you that course of conduct is sin.

Now, I do hope I have made this plain to you, my comrades, if it was not plain before. Clear ideas on the subject are necessary to your understanding so much in the plan of salvation. It is like the A B C in reading. You all know how poorly you would get along if you were not clear in the knowledge of your alphabet. You would always be making mistakes, and I am sure if you don't see distinctly what sin is, and how closely it is connected with your experience and work, you will be more or less confused in all that has to do with religion.

But I have not done yet with the subject. If you are to understand how great a blessing God's forgiveness is you must also see something of the great evil of sin.

There are many ugly things in this universe, but sin is the ugliest of them all. It is the root out of which all the other evil things upon the earth have grown. Looked at every way you choose, it is as bad as bad can be.

Sin is bad, because it is not what God intended. It is not in his plan. It is against his purpose towards our world, and therefore it hurts his feelings. He hates it, it is every day and every hour a pain to him.

Sin is bad because it makes so much misery. Look abroad, my comrades, and see this world of broken hearts and squandered fortunes and desolate homes and ruined reputations and dying men and women and half-damned souls, and then remember that all this desolation and distress are the results of sin.

Sin is bad because it leads to hell. "The soul that sinneth, it shall die." "The wicked shall be turned into hell, and all the nations that forget God."

But of this painful yet still important aspect of the case I cannot say more tonight. Another time, perhaps, it may come in for a word. But may I not ask you a question here? Do you not think that sin is a dreadful thing?

Whether regarded as the transgression of that beautiful law of love which came from the great heart of your Heavenly Father, or in full view of all the miseries with which it has cursed this poor world of ours, whether remembered while kneeling before the blessed Savior whom it brought down from Heaven and nailed to the accursed tree, or while standing on the dark cliffs that overhang the ocean of wrath, listening to the cries of the numberless souls it has plunged into the pit, we can only come to one conclusion, and that is that sin is a terrible, a dreadful thing.

I hope all listening to this letter are not only forgiven, but cleansed from every particle of this cruel thing, and that they are doing what in them lies to pull the poor sinners about them out of the fire.

II

You will remember that my last section was about the forgiveness of sin. But before I could dwell upon the blessedness of forgiveness, which is a most delightful theme, I felt that I must say something to you about the nature and character of sin. And I hope that what I did say made you feel how awful a thing it is to sin against so powerful, so just, and so loving a God.

In addition, however, to what I have already said on the subject, I want to remark that there is another feature of sin, my comrades, which makes it appear a still more serious evil, and that is the awful penalty which God has in infinite wisdom attached to it.

Now, as you know, all law has a punishment of some kind or other connected with the breach of it. Otherwise it would not be law at all. It would be no more than an expression of the wishes of those in authority. Something neither more nor less than good advice.

Eight hundred years ago, or thereabouts, there was a law in force in England that was known as the "Curfew Law." By this law it was enacted that at a certain hour of the night—sunset in summer, and eight o'clock in winter—the curfew bell should toll, on hearing which everybody must put out their fires and retire to bed, or that they should suffer some kind of pains and penalties for their disobedience.

Now, if today the government of Great Britain were to pass a similar law to that, but connected no penalty with it, I do not suppose that anyone would take any notice. The stores would open for their customers as usual, the drinking saloons would go on with their devilish business, the streetcars would go skimming along the thoroughfares, the theatres and music halls would fill and empty and the Salvation halls would witness their blessed heaven-sent sights much as they do now. No one would take any notice of the law. So far as influencing the public went, it would not be worth the parchment on which it was written, and the people for whose guidance it was intended would laugh at the whole business.

But if it was enacted by both houses of Parliament, and endorsed by King Edward, that all the people whose fires were not out, or who had not retired to rest when the curfew bell rang, were to be fined $50 or suffer a month's imprisonment, and if the government was strong enough to enforce the law it had made by the infliction of these penalties, the setting of it at naught would be looked upon as a very serious matter.

Now, the transgression of God's law has a very serious penalty attached to it, for "The wages of sin is death," and a very little thought must show anyone that whoever breaks God's law does it in the face of the possibility, nay certainty, of the penalty being inflicted, and that penalty is the everlasting loss of the soul.

There is another thing about sin which ought to make it appear a very dreadful thing to do wrong, and that is the fact that every evil act of a man's life is recorded.

I say sometimes to my audiences from the platform, "You are all sinners. You dare not stand up here and say you are not. Look over your past lives," I say, "and think of the falsehoods you have told, the cruelties you have practiced, the bad tempers you have given way to, the filthiness you have indulged in, or the drunkenness, and abominations, and blasphemies, and a heap of other evil things that you have allowed. Look at them," I say, "they are more than the hairs of your head in number. What is to be done with them? What is that you say, I ask? Do you say, 'Oh, they are all forgotten, I have forgotten them myself, and nobody will ever think of them again!'

"No, no, no," I say. "Let us suppose that long, long ago some man in this town, in a frenzied fit of revenge, follows his enemy into some dark byway and drives his knife into his heart and flees from the spot, leaving him to bleed to death where he fell. Suppose that the murderer gets clear away, and hides himself in some distant land, and that after the lapse of some ten years he returns, and you meet.

"'Hello!' you say, 'Is that you?' 'Yes, it's me,' he answers.

"'But what are you doing here?' you say. 'Oh, well,' he replies, 'I thought that I would like to see the old place, and the old faces once more.'

"'Have you come back to stay?' you ask. 'Yes, I'm going to spend the remainder of my days here, and be buried in the cemetery where my child lies.'

"'But what about that affair that happened all those years back, which led you to move off?' And suppose he answers, 'Oh, that's ancient history now, and all forgotten long ago.' 'My dear fellow,' I imagine you would say to him, 'I fancy they don't think so up at the police station. They've got your photo, and all the particulars of that event recorded up there, and if they get a hint that you're about they'll be down upon you in the twinkling of an eye. You may have forgotten this thing, but depend upon it, other people have not.'"

Just so, my comrades, the transgressions of the divine law are recorded—that is, they are written down. They are recorded in two books.

First, they are recorded in the book of a man's own memory. There are instruments at Greenwich Observatory, they tell me, which register, without human assistance, all that transpires in the weather every day of our lives. For instance, they register the density of the atmosphere, whether foggy or clear, the amount of rain or snow that falls day by day, whether the sun shines or not, and if it does shine they record the length of time he condescends to do so, together with other particulars which have to do with the changes that transpire in our climate, and in the movements of the heavenly bodies of which we know so little.

A thousand years hence, if our Lord should delay his coming till then, anyone can go to the record made by that machine, and it will tell him what sort of weather we had in England on this very day.

Now, these are wonderful instruments, but there is a far more wonderful machine in the bosom of every man and woman here. I allude to memory. That machine records the thoughts, the feelings, the actions of everyone of us, every moment of our lives, and in eternity it will repeat the story of all that has happened on earth. The idea that this is so is confirmed by the accounts we often hear of people who have fallen into the water or from some lofty height, having in a few seconds the story of their early lives, which they believed they had long since forgotten, flashed across their minds.

In every man, then, there is a book in which the things he does, whether right or wrong, register themselves. That book, if crowded with holy thoughts, loving feelings and self-sacrificing deeds for God and souls, will furnish glorious reading in the celestial City. That book, if black with the record of indulgences and passions, of neglecting God and quenching his Spirit, and the other evil things that follow in their train, will make reading calculated to increase the miseries of Hell. This is, no doubt, what the apostle means when he speaks of the worm that never dies.

Then we know that when the last trumpet has blown, and the dead have been raised, and we are all gathered before the great White Throne, one particular book will be opened, the contents of which will determine the character of the sinner's punishment, and that will be the book of God's remembrance.

All the sins of men's life-time are recorded there. God takes note of every sin a man commits. God has a long memory.

What an awful prospect lies before every human being. True, my comrades, it would be a terrible lookout for you if it were not for the glorious truth which tells us that a man's sins can be blotted out.

All that would be painful and tormenting in the recollection of our misdoings, in another world, and to a great extent in this, can be removed from the book of our own memory, while God promises to forgive and blot out all the record of the sins from his own mind. Blotting them out, that is taking them away to "remember them against us no more forever." He will not only forgive, but forget.

III

I come now to answer the very serious question: "What is to be done with it?"

1. Every man in this world is placed under the obligation to keep certain laws. I reminded you of this in a former letter. Whatever God reveals to you by his Word, or by his Holy Spirit, or by your own conscience to be your duty either to him or your fellows, that is God's law for you.

2. The transgression of that law, as we have seen, is sin, and I am sure you will see at a glance that in some way or other it must be dealt with.

Looked at from any conceivable standpoint, it must appear to you that God could not leave it unnoticed. To begin with, there was his own honor. What would be thought of any earthly father, who allowed his children to keep or break the rules he made for their guidance, just as they took it into their heads? They would despise such a parent, and say, "Oh, he's nobody, and you need not take any notice of him." And all who knew of such a state of things would despise him, too.

Just so, if our Heavenly Father allowed men to carry out his wishes, or go contrary to them according to their fancy or their feelings, without either rewards or punishments, they would despise him.

3. You will see also, if you give the matter a little thought, that God must deal with sin, or his law would lose its hold on the respect of those for whom it has been made. If men were allowed to break the law as they please, without suffering for it, the result would soon be the same as if there was no law, and a world without law would be little better than a hell.

4. The benevolent regard which God has for all his creatures binds him to deal with the transgressions of his laws. Only think of the state of wretchedness and helplessness to which the people of any country would soon be reduced, if the laws that have to do with the protection of life and property could be broken with impunity.

All the thieves and rascals in that country would at once come to the front, and the weak people would be robbed and wronged until life would become a burden too grievous to be borne.

Just so, no one can imagine how awful would have been the anarchy and woe that would have spread itself throughout God's great Kingdom if the sin of Adam and all the people who have followed in his track had not been dealt with. God, as the Governor of the creatures he has made, is under the most solemn obligation to take notice of sin.

Well, now, if sin had to be dealt with, how was it to be done? There were only two ways. One way was to punish it by the infliction of the penalty on the transgressor, and that penalty was death, and the other way was to forgive him.

The infliction of the penalty man had deserved would, doubtless, have secured each of the ends I have mentioned. Angels, devils, and men would all agree that it would have maintained the honor of God, exalted the law in the eyes of his creatures, and generally promoted the well-being of the universe. But God chose another plan. Instead of punishing sin he made a way for its forgiveness.

He made an exhibition before Heaven, earth, and hell, of the dignity of the law he had enacted, the importance of obedience to it, and the great evil of breaking it, by giving his Son Jesus Christ to die on Calvary, and at the same time opened the gates of forgiveness to every son and daughter of Adam's race.

From that day to this, no being anywhere has been able to say that it is a light matter to oppose God, or to break his commandments. And yet on the cross there was the strongest assertion possible for any being to make, of the possibility of full and free forgiveness for every sinner who is willing to comply with the conditions on which its bestowment is made to depend.

1. Now, what do we mean by "The forgiveness of sin?" I answer. "It is that act wherein God does for his Son our Savior's sake fully and freely forgive all the sins of a man's past life, on the simple condition of repentance and faith in our Lord Jesus Christ."

You will see that this is not the covering up of sins with the good works of Jesus Christ, as some have thought. Neither does forgiveness consist in treating a man, for Christ's sake, as though he had never sinned, but, while regarding him as the guilty, hell-deserving sinner he really is, it means the complete forgiveness of all the transgression of which he has been guilty.

2. The forgiveness of sin is the definite act of God. It is a transaction that takes place between the soul and God himself.

You cannot forgive your own sins. You may hate them, repent of them, and renounce them, all of which you ought to do, all of which you must do, but you cannot forgive them.

No other man or number of men can forgive your sins. Neither priest, nor church, nor officer, nor all the good people on the earth, nor all the angelic beings in Heaven, could forgive you, were they all to join hands together for that purpose. He only can forgive the sin against whom the sin has been committed. It is God who forgives sin, and God alone.

The Bible cannot save you. Some people seem to think that it can. They think that if you believe some words or text, or some doctrine taught in it, you will be forgiven. That is a mistake. The most that the Scriptures can do is to point out the way of salvation. They can say, "Behold the Lamb of God, that taketh away the sins of the world!" but only God can take the sins away, so, if you have not already done so, go to him direct this very day, and let him do this for you.

This is the doctrine of the Bible. The prophet Isaiah said: "Let the wicked forsake his way, and the unrighteous man his thoughts, and let him return unto the Lord and he will have mercy upon him, and to our God, for he will abundantly pardon." And John the apostle wrote those wonderful words: "He is faithful and just to forgive us our sins, and to cleanse us from all unrighteousness."

The publican in the temple of whom Jesus Christ spoke did not call on either the priest or the congregation for forgiveness: he cried, "God be merciful to me a sinner," and went home with his sins forgiven.

This doctrine is set forth and maintained by the testimony of holy men of God in all ages everywhere. Not only from the lips of the Psalmist, but throughout the Army in all lands you will hear men and women bear witness that they cried to the Lord, and he brought them out of the horrible pit, and set their feet on the rock, and put a new song into their mouths, even praise and thanksgiving to God.

This is the doctrine, my comrades, of your own experience. You remember well when weighed down by your sins and afraid of death, and judgment, and eternity on account of them, you sought deliverance from the Lord, and it was God himself who came to your relief, and who spoke your sins forgiven. Every Salvationist should settle this truth deep and immovable in his soul. It will help him in the perplexities and difficult situations that lie before him, to remember that forgiveness is of the Lord. It is God that saves.

2. The forgiveness of sins is entire. That is to say, the act covers the whole of the wrong-doings of a man's past life. Some people feel that it is too much to expect God to forgive all their sins at once. Even when they have the courage to believe that God will forgive them at all, they cannot bring themselves to believe that it can be done all at one sweep.

They think that God forgives sins in the same manner that some creditors forgive the liabilities of some poor debtor—that is, by drawing his pen through a few pages of the list against him on one day, and a few more the next, and so on. In this way they imagine God deals with the long record of the evil doings of a sinner. Forgiving, first, for instance, the sins of his youth, and then the sins of his early manhood, and so on to the end.

No, this is not our Father's way! As some old writer has it: "God's plan is not to cross out this lot of debts now, and another lot the day after, and another lot the day after, but to turn the inkstand upside down on the record, blotting them out altogether."

Was not this the way the father forgave his prodigal son? Was there any doing the thing by halves there? Let us see. Did he say to the broken-hearted youth: "First, I shall forgive you all the naughty things you did before you went away, and then I will pardon the wretched things you did while you were away, and by and by I will deal with the ingratitude you practiced in refusing to come home when I invited you?" No, he ran to meet him, and putting his arms around him, took him to his heart, and forgave all at a stroke.

Jesus Christ uses that earthly father's compassion and forgiveness to set forth before our eyes the compassion and forgiveness of our Heavenly Father. That is the way God pardons sins. Oh, my comrades, that is the way he pardons you, and that is the way he pardoned me fifty-seven years ago, and that is the forgiveness of which I have the witness in my own heart at the present time. I hope that every one of you have the witness of that blessed forgiveness in yours also. If not, if there should be one among you who has it not, now is the accepted time, behold this is the day of salvation.

10

About Being Saved—Conversion

YOU WILL REMEMBER THAT the purpose of this part is to show you what we Salvationists mean when we talk about being saved.

I have dealt with the blessing of "forgiveness," and I now want to have a talk with you about "conversion," which is, in my estimation, an equally important theme. Indeed, I am not sure whether as a subject it is not even more important to us as a people in particular, and to the world in general, than forgiveness, because it seems of late to have dropped so very much out of notice in the bulk of the churches. I fear that you will very seldom hear the topic mentioned outside our borders.

Many preachers and writers have much to say about the love of God, and the death of Christ, and the desirability of being good, and just, and true, but very few dwell particularly or frequently on the subject of that "new heart" which is created by the Holy Spirit, and of which the Savior spoke so plainly. And yet without its possession anything like true spiritual joy and holy living are simply impossible. And alas! even where conversion is commonly spoken of, and professedly believed in, I am afraid that the notions respecting it are often very mistaken, and in some cases positively false and misleading.

This applies, I am afraid, to some Salvationists, and to make them understand better what it is to be converted is one of the objects of this chapter.

Now you will know that to be converted is to be changed. It is to be made different from what you were before. If a man goes to the mercy-seat, or kneels down in his own chamber and repents of his sins, and exercises saving faith in Christ, he will be converted. What does this mean? What has happened to the man who has been converted? Let me try and show you this.

1. Let me say that conversion does not consist in a change of opinions. A change of opinions, and that often to a very remarkable extent, follows conversion, if it does not actually accompany it, but it does not constitute conversion. Many unconverted people learn a great deal more than the converted people do. There can be any amount of knowledge about what is right and what is wrong, about God, and Jesus Christ, and duty, and indeed about almost every other religious subject, without conversion.

In the seventh chapter of Romans we have a description of a man whose head is full of knowledge, but whose heart has not been changed. That is, a man who, though concerned about religion, has not been converted. He sees the sort of life he ought to live, he desires it, condemns himself because he does not realize it, but he has not the power to act up to his conviction of duty. He has the light, but has not the ability required to walk in it. He cries out, "The good that I would, I do not: but the evil which I would not, that I do." He knows his Master's will, but does it not. What is he to do? Is he merely to get to know that will more perfectly? No, his first duty is to seek the power to do it. He will get that in conversion.

Neither does a change of doctrine or belief always mean conversion. For instance, a man may change over from being a Roman Catholic to being a Protestant, or from being a heathen to being a Christian, and if it is only a change of belief to which he attains, he will be very little, if any, nearer to the heart of Jesus Christ and the life of the Spirit than he was before. There is nothing gained by holding the truth in unrighteousness.

2. Conversion does not consist merely in a change of bodily habits. When those habits have been evil, conversion will insure such a change, and that in a most remarkable degree. It is quite common amongst us, as you will know, for men who have been the slaves of drink and opium, and of many other evil indulgences, to lose the unnatural appetite for those things at the moment of their conversion, but still a man can even overcome these slavish things and yet stop short of being converted.

3. Conversion is not repentance. Repentance is a condition of conversion, but it is possible to repent without going on to the realization of that marvelous change which we are speaking of.

A man may be very sorry about his past sins, and go to the penitent-form, and weep, and pray, and be forgiven, yet never be converted.

There is little doubt about that being the actual history of multitudes of the people we see about us, who are off and on with religion all the time. God is always waking them up by death-beds, sicknesses or losses, by strivings of his Spirit, and appeals from the platform. On these occasions they weep, and pray, and promise, and then directly afterwards go back to the same state that they were in before. They are penitent, sincerely penitent for the time, but they stop short of getting converted, and so, being just as weak as they were before, they naturally relapse into their former condition.

4. Conversion is not forgiveness. Forgiveness of sin always goes with it, indeed, when you think about conversion you think about forgiveness at the same time. They are twin blessings, and walk into a man's soul at the same moment, forgiveness leading the way. But although so nearly related, and always found together, they differ materially.

If you could have one without the other you would find a great difference. You can easily imagine that a man might have all his past sins pardoned, have a clean slate, as it were, but if that were all, when the nice feelings had passed, and the old temptations came, he being the same man, would fall into the same or similar sins, and soon pile up a new record similar to that just washed away. He wants to be made a different man in order to lead a different life. That is, he needs conversion.

Forgiveness is something that God does outside of a man. Conversion is something that he does inside of him. In forgiveness he blots out the record of his transgressions, saves him from the condemnation of sin, writes his name in the Book of Life, and makes him a citizen of the New Jerusalem. In conversion he changes his nature, makes him hate the evil things that before he hated. Conversion and forgiveness go together, they are never parted—but they are not the same.

5. Conversion is the doctrine of the Bible. All the teaching of Jesus Christ and his apostles proceeds on the assumption that the real Christian has undergone a change of heart. Jesus Christ taught this truth explicitly when he said, "Except a man be born again, he cannot see the kingdom of God... That which is born of the flesh is flesh, and that which is born of the Spirit is Spirit. Marvel not that I said unto thee, Ye must be

born again." And again, when he said, "Except ye be converted, and become as little children, ye shall not enter into the Kingdom of Heaven."

The sum of this teaching is—first, that to become a child of God, a man must experience an inward change so real and great as to be comparable to being born afresh, secondly, this change can only be effected by the power of the Holy Spirit, and thirdly, that without it no man can possess the life or experience or the blessings, or have the power enjoyed by the members of the Kingdom of Heaven in this world or in the world to come. Conversion is a wonderful experience, and it is an absolute necessity.

To be converted then, is to have a change of heart. And with a changed heart there will be a changed life. The heart controls and determines the character of the life. Selfish, proud, revengeful, ambitious, worldly, devilish hearts make it impossible for those who possess them to live other than selfish, proud, revengeful, ambitious, worldly, devilish lives. Just so, pure, and humble, and benevolent, in short, Christ-like lives. If our hearts are like Christ, then our conduct will be Christ-like also.

11

About Being Saved—Evidences of Salvation

IN THE PRESENT AGE which claims the possession of many things superior to those enjoyed in the past, you will hear the cry on all hands, "Proof, proof, give us proof of the reality of what you claim."

This is not an unreasonable demand. I earnestly wish there was more of the same spirit in connection with religion. Anyway, when a man stands up saying: "I have had a transaction with God himself, I have knelt at his feet, I have heard his voice, he has forgiven my sins and made me a new creature, he enables me to live a new, a holy, a heavenly life," it is reasonable that evidences of so marvelous a fact should be asked for.

No man ought to conclude that he is in a state of salvation, or expect those around him to believe that he is, without proof of the fact. Can satisfactory evidences be produced? I am sure they can, and I propose to name several in this chapter.

In doing so I may repeat some of the truths I have already referred to in these chapters. I have no doubt I shall. But I cannot help that, my aim is not so much to produce something new every time I write to you, as to impress truth of everlasting importance on your minds and hearts.

I am not proposing to refer at this time to every proof that can be furnished as to the possession of salvation, but I do hope that you will carefully consider those that I do mention, and that you will conscientiously ask yourself the question "Is that true of me?"

1. The first evidence which I have to name is that which arises from a man's feeling that the experience to which I have referred has already transpired in his own soul. This is what we call consciousness.

The soul knows that it has salvation because it remembers the act of forgiveness taking place, and has a sense of God's favor at the present moment. If there is not an exact recollection of the time and place when the transition from death unto life took place, there is the blessed consciousness that it has really occurred, and the actual realization that it is now the fact.

This inward feeling, which enables us to look to Heaven and cry out "Abba, Father, my Lord and my God," is the most convincing evidence a man can possibly have of his own salvation. Nothing is more satisfying to the Salvationist himself, or more unanswerable to the stranger who proposes the question, "What makes you think you are saved?" than to be able to answer back again, "because I know it."

This consciousness is spoken of in the Bible by the word "know." Thus Job says, "I know that my Redeemer liveth." Paul says, "I know whom I have believed." John says, "He that believeth on the Son of God hath the witness in himself," and also "Hereby we know that we are of the truth, and shall assure our hearts before him. . . .Beloved, if our heart condemn us not, then have we confidence toward God."

This "knowing" is only another word for "realization," and means consciousness, that is, "I feel that it is so," it is the work of the Spirit of God, and it constitutes the most convincing evidence of salvation possible to man.

A sincere man may have sufficient knowledge of his Bible and of the plan of salvation to enable him to say, "I think I am saved."

And he may go further still, and be able to say, "I hope I am saved." Nay, he may go further still, and say, "I believe I am saved."

But he may—blessed be God!—go far beyond all this, and say "I know I am saved." Then he can sing—

> *I am saved, I am saved,*
> *Jesus bids me go free,*
> *I am washed in the Blood,*
> *Even me, even me.*

But not only is consciousness the most convincing evidence of the actual possession of salvation that a man can possess, it is probably the only evidence that can create satisfaction in the soul on this all-important question. Without it, no matter what thought is expended, or what knowledge is acquired, no matter what hopes may be cherished, or what truths may be believed, the soul will never rest. Only this can make a man unquestionably at peace on the subject of his own salvation.

I do not say that there is no salvation without the inward realization. I do not say that every man is to doubt the safety of his neighbor or fear the reality of his own safety who does not possess it. But I do say that for a man to feel that his Heavenly Father is reconciled to him, and does really and truly save him at the present moment, is a most convincing and most satisfying, and therefore valuable evidence of the possession of salvation. And, thank God, this evidence is within the reach of everyone.

2. Another evidence of salvation is the confession of it. By which I mean a becoming and resolute acknowledgment before friends and foes that you are not only on the side of Jehovah and his people and his truth, but that God has, for Christ's sake, forgiven your sins and taken you into his family and made you one of his disciples.

Such a confession appears most reasonable. If you were in Heaven you would be proud to hoist your colors and to tell all the inhabitants of that World of Light that you belonged to God. Why, then, not here in your family, or workshop, or wherever your lot may be cast? It may be a little difficult, it may cost you something, but the usefulness of such an acknowledgment cannot be called in question. God expects it of you, and it is at your peril that you withhold it. Jesus Christ said, "If any man be ashamed of Me and my words, in this generation, of him will I be ashamed when I come in the glory of my Father, and with all his holy angels."

While not judging other people, I do not see how you can walk before your Lord with any semblance of reality, if you are ashamed of your Father, and of being a follower of the Lamb.

3. Another evidence of salvation is the possession of a new and Christlike purpose in life. Unconverted men live in one way or another to please themselves. Self is the idol they set up within their souls, and this they worship and obey all the time. Some seek the gratification of this god by one means and some by others.

Some, for example, seek to gratify themselves by acquiring money, others by running after pleasure, others by coveting and striving for the admiration of their fellows, and others seek it in religion. They go to the synagogues, or read their Bibles, or say their prayers, or sing hymns, just to please themselves. With the whole of this fraternity it is Self, Self, what "I like,"—morning, noon, and night they serve the self-god.

The saved man has been converted, and evidences it by abandoning this devotion to self, and coming over to the service of Jesus Christ. He lives, not to please himself, but to please his Heavenly Father, and bless his fellowmen.

Now the true Salvationist may do this in a very blundering and imperfect manner, but still, love to God and the desire to please him is the ruling purpose of his soul. Thereby he proves to himself and to those about him that he is really and truly in a state of salvation.

And if this is not the case, if he is still ruled by desires for his own gratification, then, no matter what may be his profession, Paul clearly sets forth what is his real state when he says—

"Though I speak with the tongues of men and of angels, and have not charity (love), I am become as sounding brass, or a tinkling cymbal . . . And though I bestow all my goods to feed the poor, and though I give my body to be burned, and have not charity (love), it profiteth me nothing."

I have further evidences of this wonderful salvation yet to speak of, but I want you each to search out whether these proofs of which I have spoken mark your own experience and profession of salvation.

12

About Being Saved—Further Evidences of Salvation

I CONCLUDED MY LAST chapter when writing of a most important part of my subject. I was speaking of the evidences by which a man can judge whether he is in a state of salvation or not. I named three of them, each in my estimation being very important.

The first was the personal realization of the fact. A truly saved man knows that he is saved. To what I have said on that point let me add that this sense of certainty is the result not only of a man's knowledge that he has complied with the conditions laid down in the Bible, that he has turned to God and submitted to his claims, and then by faith claimed forgiveness and conversion, but it is the work of the Holy Ghost given to him to assure him that his action has been acceptable to God, and that his past sins are forgiven, and that he is admitted into the divine family. It is of this that Paul speaks when he says, "The Spirit itself beareth witness with our spirit, that we are the children of God."

The second evidence I mentioned was the open avowal of the fact. If Christ has been formed in the heart of a man, he will not hesitate to boldly say so. If a man has taken his stand for God and righteousness, he will acknowledge the side he is on before the world around him, and the world will know it.

The third proof of salvation which I named to you was the fact that a saved man comes under the ruling power of love. Love to God, and love to man become the great purpose of his life. Unsaved men live to please themselves. Saved men live to please God and to bless men.

I now come to speak of further evidences. They are very numerous, but I can only find space here to mention a few. In addition to those already given, I want you to think of the following:

1. If a man is saved he will live a good life. He will exhibit what the Bible calls "the fruits of the Spirit."

He will be a man of truth—that is, he will not only abstain from telling lies, but will not permit himself in the practice of any deceit, either in speech or action. You know people can act an untruth as well as deliberately speak that which they know to be false, but all such is inconsistent with a state of salvation. The devil is spoken of as the "great deceiver," and those who follow him in the practice of any kind of deception cannot regard themselves as the children of God.

Honesty also will be a feature of the life of a good man. You would not be found, my comrades, putting your hand into your employer's till, or into your neighbor's pocket to take money, but do you equally recognize that a servant who wastes his employer's time is just as dishonest as those who steal from his cash-box? In all his relationships, whether in great or in little things, the principle of honesty will govern the man or woman who is really saved.

Industry and attention to duty are inseparable from good living. Laziness is out of harmony with any profession of holiness. The truly good man will take trouble with himself and the work which comes to his hands. He will not only do that which he has undertaken to do, but will seek to do it in the best way, so as to secure the best results. He will be properly described in the Bible words as being "diligent in business" as well as "fervent in spirit."

I must remind you also that good living includes kindness. Life is full of opportunities for actions of this sort. An encouraging word will be spoken here, a helping hand given there, little obstacles will be removed out of the path of the weak and stumbling ones, and the ministering spirit of kindness will show itself at every turn.

You see I am not stopping to describe these qualities fully. I only want to show you some of the signs of goodness which must come out in the life of a saved man. He will manifest these virtues, not only in his own family, but in all his relations with his fellows. He will thus let his light so shine before men that they, seeing his good works, will glorify his Father which is in Heaven. Imperfect he may be, faulty in many particulars, but in the main he will be seen and known by those around him to be a good man.

2. A saved man will care for the salvation of his fellows. I have already said that he will love to seek to bless others, but in particular he

will have his senses awakened to the value of men's souls. I do not see how any man can claim to be in a state of salvation who does not possess at least a measure of the spirit of Jesus in this respect. As Paul said, "If any man have not the spirit of Christ, he is none of his." What was that spirit? Not only submission to his Father's will and the exhibition of a beautiful and holy disposition, but the spirit which spared not himself when his very life had to be sacrificed for the redemption of men.

3. Another evidence of salvation is the ability to live by faith. I mean to say that whilst worldly-minded and unsaved people are influenced in all they do by their natural senses, saved men regulate their lives by spiritual senses—that is, by a belief in great truths and facts, such as the love and power and claims of a God and Savior, and eternal realities not discerned by physical eyes or ears or touch. They walk by faith.

> *Faith lends its realizing light,*
> *The clouds disperse, the shadows fly,*
> *The Invisible appears in sight,*
> *And God is seen by mortal eye.*

Like Moses, the saved man endures "as seeing him who is invisible." This brings to him the assurance of God's providential care. Believing that the steps of a good man are ordered by the Lord, he knows that all things will work together for his good. And, still further, he is strengthened in the midst of the battles of life by the assurance of ultimate victory and glorious reward.

4. The saved man enjoys an abiding peace, which of itself is a strong evidence of this salvation. He is at peace as regards the past, knowing that his guilt has been washed away by the blood of Christ. He has peace as regards God, for has he not received the inward assurance of divine favor, and the witness that his ways please God? And as regards the great future, with its Resurrection Morn and Judgment Throne, the saved man views all with a soul kept in peace by God himself.

5. The saved man also enjoys divine communion. By that I mean more than if I had said "he prays." Even the sinner can pray, and pray acceptably, "God be merciful to me a sinner," but the saved man knows that he is saved when, in addition to prayer and supplication for himself

and others, he can enjoy divine intercourse as of a child with its father, or of a friend with friend. If you are properly saved, you are of the company who can truthfully say, "Our fellowship is with the Father, and with his Son Jesus Christ."

6. Saved men and women give evidence of the fact by their perseverance. That is to say, the blessings of salvation have become so real and precious to them that they find satisfaction in following on to know and do the will of God, turning from worldly pleasure and selfish indulgences, which would be likely to hinder them and damage their influence with those around them, and leaving "the things which are behind, and reaching forth unto those things which are before," they "press toward the mark for the prize of the high calling of God in Christ Jesus."

At the same time, I must remind you, my comrades, that none of these experiences and joys lift you to a state from which it is impossible to fall. Many, alas! have turned aside almost from the very gate of Heaven, and have gone down to the backslider's misery on earth, and the backslider's hell hereafter. And whilst rejoicing with you over the possession of the evidences of salvation which I have described, I counsel you to watch and pray lest you enter into the temptations surrounding you, to take heed to yourselves in all things, for the more earnestly you do this and press forward, the more certain is it that you will not turn back, and thus lose all the blessings that Jesus Christ has already given you.

13

Prayer

So closely allied is this subject to your peace, power, and usefulness, that I feel constrained to say something on the theme. In this chapter I want to speak of the manner in which you should approach God in order to secure the blessings you desire.

To be able to pray so as not only to reach the ear and move the heart of God, but to insure the bestowment of the blessings for which you ask, is a very wonderful gift.

God has manifested the satisfaction with which he regards that kind of prayer by the marvelous answers he has given to it all the way down the stream of history. All good men enjoy a measure of the gift, and covet much more.

Bad men fear it, and stand in dread of those whom they have reason to believe possess it. The fervent effectual prevailing prayer of which the apostle James speaks is altogether a wonderful thing. Of it the old hymn writer says:

> *Prayer makes the darkest cloud withdraw,*
> *Prayer climbs the ladder Jacob saw,*
> *And Satan trembles when he sees*
> *The weakest saint upon his knees.*

I

To try and show to you how you can offer that kind of prayer is, then, the object of this chapter. My task is rather difficult. I need not say that you will make little progress unless you already possess that spirit which comes with the new heart, and which causes the soul to cry out, "Abba, Father, my Lord and my God." I shall assume that you possess this divine instinct, and that you do here and now join me in the request:

O thou by whom we come to God,
The Life, the Truth, the Way!
The path of prayer thyself hast trod:
Lord! teach us how to pray.

There are different kinds of prayer—that is to say, occasion, and the circumstances of those offering prayer differing, render the character of their prayers different. The prayer of the publican in the temple, and the dying cry of the thief on the cross were called forth by different circumstances from that of Elijah when he lay prostrate on Mount Carmel calling on God for rain on the dried-up hills and valleys of Judea.

Now, I want specially to speak of what we call private prayer—that is, the prayer that every one of you soldiers may be supposed to offer day by day, say every morning or evening. Such prayer ought, I think, to have in it seven different points. You might call it a ladder of seven different rounds, reaching from earth to heaven, up which every soldier climbs, as I have said, into the very presence of his Maker every day.

1. Now, the first round of my ladder I will call reality. That is be real, be in earnest when you seek to approach God. Beware of formality! In no exercise of religion is there more danger of formality than in prayer, and in no exercise is formality a greater enemy of usefulness. Beware of it! Shake yourself up by reminding yourself that you are going into the very presence of God in order that you may speak directly to him on matters that concern not only your own highest well-being, but that of those nearest and dearest to you.

Perhaps you may say, "Am I not always in the presence of God?" Yes, you are, and you cannot by any scheming go away from his Spirit, for in him you live and move and have your being. But still, the soul can by its own choice and purpose enter into the Holy of Holies and come more particularly to his sacred feet.

That is what is done in real prayer, and you do not want to engage in the form of prayer unless it is a real coming before God. Therefore impress this on your mind.

And you may also say to me, "Does not the apostle tell me that I am to be always praying?" Yes, he does. He says, "Pray without ceasing," which I take to mean that you are to live all the time in the spirit of holy communion with your Heavenly Father. That is to live so that your prayer shall never be out of harmony with your feelings.

But then the duties of your daily life, and the lawful anxieties you are compelled to feel about the Salvation War and other things, must necessarily occupy your attention to a great extent. But when you wish specially to commune with God you must turn aside, as Moses did in the wilderness, to do so. You will remember that he took off his shoes, and spoke to God, who appeared to him in the burning bush. If you turn aside from your cares and anxieties, and prostrate yourself before God in the same spirit he will hear your petitions and answer them. Therefore remind yourself of the importance of the action when you bow yourself to pray.

Then you must begin your prayers by putting your soul into actual communion with God. When I approach God I never feel that I am really praying until I am able to realize that I have, as it were, attracted the attention of God, and that I am speaking actually to him, and that he is listening to what I say. This is what I sometimes call, in a telegraphic phrase, being "switched on."

Perhaps you will know that when you want to speak to anyone in some distant town through the telephone, you ask the central office exchange to connect the wire through which you are speaking with the wire of the office or home of the party with whom you want to converse. Then, being connected, you call his attention and your conversation takes place. Now, something answering to this should take place in your soul, only that in such a case it is yourself that wants waking up, and it is yourself that wants connecting with your Heavenly Father, seeing that he is ever on the lookout for your approach and his ear is ever open to your cry.

You can take a simpler illustration. When you want to speak to the captain about any matter which has to do with the corps, or some comrade who is sick, or some soul whom you want to win, you don't go outside his quarters and begin to shout out your business, or ask him to render you such service as you desire. Supposing that he was at the open window listening, you would have no pleasure in talking at random into the air. No, you would want to feel that he was there, and listening to you, and preparing to answer you back as you desire.

Just so with God. If you are to put any reality into your prayer, you must feel after God and believe in God, and cast yourself on God right at the beginning, and you won't have long to wait before he answers your cry, and makes you feel that you are talking to his heart. And the promise shall be verified in your experience: "Before you call, he will answer, and while you are yet speaking, he will hear."

2. The second step in my golden ladder is worship. By which I mean adoration, thanksgiving, praise. You believe that he is the great God—almighty, all-wise, all-loving, your Creator, your Redeemer, your Father, your Friend. Speak to him of his greatness, bow yourself before him, and it will do you good, and encourage you in the exercise on which you have entered.

Thank him for all the mercies he has bestowed upon you and those you love and care about. When you kneel down in the morning you should think upon all the health and strength and preservation and the blessing of all kinds you asked him for the previous night, and when you kneel down at night remember the blessings you asked from him in the morning. If they have been given you, this is the moment for gratitude. You cannot do less than thank him for the display of so much love. Well, do it.

II

You will remember that, in speaking of prayer in my last section, I compared it to a ladder reaching from earth to heaven, and composed of seven distinct parts, which I compared to seven golden stairs.

I did not say that these seven stairs represented all the important parts of prayer—far from it. Still I did then, and do now, set them forth as being very important features, which should be diligently sought after when we go aside with God to engage in the delightful exercise of prayer.

Of the seven rounds in this wonderful ladder I noticed two.

1. The first I called "reality," by which I meant that you were to be real and in earnest when you seek to approach God, and that you were to beware of formality.

2. The second point I noted was "worship," by which I meant the adoration of God as your God, and thanking him for all the blessings that

are continually being bestowed upon you.

3. I now come to the third point, which I will name "petition"—that is, the presentation to God of the requests you have to make. Here I would remind you of what I have said before, that although in praying you are talking to the greatest Being in the universe, you cannot be too simple or natural in what you have to say to him.

He wants you to approach him as his children, and is delighted for you to use the simplest words that you can find to express your wishes and describe your needs. So do not be afraid to talk out your hearts before him as though you were talking to a friend who understood all about you.

Some have been a little puzzled as to whether it is best to pray aloud, when we pray alone, or simply to ask with the silent inward desires of the mind. If my opinion were asked on the subject I should certainly say—if circumstances allow—use your voice. This plan seems to be favored by the Scriptures. You are to "ask and receive," and to open your mouth wide for God to fill it. And we can be quite sure that the publican in the temple lifted up his voice, or Christ would not have heard him.

So, although I am not laying down any fixed rule, I advise that when convenient you use your lips, if for no other reason than that the spoken prayer is most likely to help your heart by stirring up its emotions and helping its faith.

But, my comrades, whether you raise your voice, or simply pray with the silent cry of your heart, ask God plainly and definitely for what you want. To pray at all supposes that there is something you want God to do for you. If you don't need anything, don't pray, for unless you need something and want God to supply that need, prayer is useless for man and a mockery to God.

But perhaps you will say, "Why should I tell God about my needs, does he not know all about them?" Yes, doubtless he does. He knows them a great deal better than you know them yourself. He says so. "Your Heavenly Father knoweth what things ye have need of before ye ask him."

But if you want him to supply those needs, he has willed that you should go to his feet and ask him to do so. The reason why it should be so

I will refer to in another letter. Meanwhile I say, bring your petitions to God and definitely and boldly present them.

(a) Ask for the supply of what you need for yourself.

For your body that it may be fed and clothed and generally cared for. If you are in health, ask him to keep you well. If you are sick, ask him to heal you, if it be his blessed will.

Ask him to supply the need of your mind and of your heart. You will be sure every day to have some joy or some sorrow, some hope or some fear, some temptation or some triumph, with which you will be more or less exercised. Whatever it may be, bring it before your Lord, seek his aid, he will be pleased to help you, if you ask him to do so.

(b) Ask him to supply your family needs. Those nearest to us by earthly relationship have the first claim on our sympathy and intercession at the throne. When my dear wife was alive, her name was ever the first breathed from my lips at that sacred hour.

Then, the children will come along. They ever bring love and joy with them, and all the way, till you lay them in the grave, or until they lay you there, they bring care and anxiety as well. With some it is more, and with others less, but, in any case, they will furnish an object for your intercession at the throne of grace.

Day by day, when bowed before my Heavenly Father, I bring my children before him, running through their names one by one, including the husbands or wives and children of those who are married, spreading out their needs at the hour, so far as I know them.

It will be so with you, my comrades. Those bound most closely to us by the ties of flesh and blood must have a first claim on our hearts when we have access to the Holy Place.

(c) After your family will come your comrades. Your officers, with any particular difficulties with which they may be battling, your corps, with its warfare against the devil and sin, and your comrades all have a claim on your prayers that you cannot pass by.

In my private devotions I usually pass from my relations according to the flesh, to my brothers and sisters according to the Spirit, and in order that I may not leave any out I take them rank by rank, beginning with the commissioners and finishing up with the soldiers—nay, for the hearers as well, who sit unsaved in our halls. I am not happy unless I feel that I have embraced every department of the war, and everyone engaged in it.

(d) In your secret communion with God you must not forget the poor sinners of your own particular neighborhood, nor the heathen crowds amongst whom our precious flag flies. Somebody should plead for them. Why not you?

I was reading only lately of a very poor woman who sat in the back seat of the meeting, of whom nobody took much notice, and for whom nobody seemed to care. But she was well saved and loved God and souls. It was her custom to pick out some young man who occasionally came to the place and pray for his conversion until she had the joy of seeing him saved. By persevering in this course it was found on her dying bed that twenty men had been converted and made into faithful soldiers of Jesus Christ.

Then there is the world at large and other matters connected with your own lot transpiring every day, which will call for your prayers. O my comrades, you must pray!

4. I now come to the fourth step in my golden stair, and that is, your prayer must be offered in the Savior's name. Your prayers should be specially addressed to your Heavenly Father, but they should be presented in the name of Jesus Christ your Savior, and the answer requested and expected for his dear sake.

I hope you see the force of this arrangement, my comrades! Let me try and illustrate it to you. Here is a father, we will suppose, who has a son whom he values very highly. The son goes off to a distant land on some important business for his father, where he forms a friendship for some other young man. This friend falls ill, and he nurses him back to life. In doing so he contracts the disease, which proves fatal. On his dying bed he says to his friend, "I am dying. I cannot stay to help you, as my heart would wish, in the trials which will come upon you as you travel through life. But when difficulties arise you must appeal to my father. He loves me much. He is rich, and for my sake he will help you."

So, my comrades, Jesus Christ loves you, and gave himself for you even unto death. His Father loves him, and when you want help you have the privilege of mentioning his name, and for his sake God will answer your prayer.

There is another illustration which will help some who may read this letter better to understand why they should present their petitions in the name of our dear Savior. An old-fashioned writer says: "When you send your prayers to heaven, be sure and direct them to the care of your Redeemer, and they will never miscarry."

Another says: "When I ask my Father to receive my prayer through Jesus Christ my Lord, I feel that I put my prayer into Jesus Christ's hands."

Suppose you had to draw up a petition to the king, and you had never done such a thing before, you would be afraid of making twenty blunders. But suppose that the Prince of Wales said to you, "Put it into my hands, and what is wrong I will put out, and what is wanting I will put in, and I will put my own name to it, and present it for you to my father the king." Would not a petition drawn up in that way and presented after that fashion be likely to gain the attention of the king?

Now, when I present my requests to God, imperfect and ignorant as I am, I am likely to pray for twenty wrong things, Christ gives me permission to put them into his hands and he puts all the blunders out, and puts in all that is wanted, and puts his own name to it, and presents it to his Father.

Comrades, pray on, pray more than ever, and offer your prayers in the name of Jesus Christ, and he will put them right, and present them to his Father, the King of kings.

14

Prayer—Submission to God

WE ARE STILL AT work on the golden stairway that leads to the mercy seat. I want you to love prayer, and to cultivate the habit of praying. There are many reasons why you should do so. Among others, because of its blessed effects on your own hearts, and because of the wonderful changes it can bring about for your comrades and the world at large.

The saints of old, and the Salvationists of our own times, received, and still receive, wonderful answers to their intercessions, and they were men and women of like passions with ourselves. Why should you not accomplish similar marvels at the mercy-seat? There is no reason on earth or in heaven why it should not be so.

To help you in this hilly exercise I will proceed with my subject. Of the seven rounds of the golden ladder we are describing we have already spoken of four.

5. The fifth is "desire," and was spoken of by the Savior when he said, "Whatsoever things ye desire when ye pray, believing that ye receive them and ye shall have them." It would be little less than a mockery to ask God for what we do not desire him to bestow upon us.

6. The sixth step is "submission," by which I mean that your prayers must, so far as you can discover, be always in harmony with your Father's will.

Therefore, while you ask God to give you what you wish for, what you think is good for you, what you think he ought to give you, nevertheless you can only ask that he will give it you if he sees that it will be best for you and most likely to promote his glory.

You are fallible and may make mistakes. He may see that what you ask him for will really injurious to you or opposed to the welfare of others.

For instance, I will suppose that you are a farmer or a gardener and want rain. But God might see that rain just now would not be good for your farm or your garden, and that you may get better crops in the long run without it, or that rain may not be good for your near neighbor, whose interests he has to consider as well as yours. Therefore he will not give you rain. Or here is a mother watching by what appears to be the dying bed of her child. The dear mother naturally wants her boy to live, but God may see that if he lives he will fall into dreadful sins and break her heart. So her prayers may not be answered.

Or you may be tried with poverty or affliction or disappointment, and you may ask God to come to your help and deliver you, but he may see that you are likely to be happier, more useful, and more likely to finish up in heaven with these trials and losses than without them. Therefore he feels it best to refuse your prayers and leave you to struggle with your afflictions while he promises you grace sufficient for them all.

Now, what does all this teach us? I think it makes plain that when we pray, unless we know what God's mind is about the things for which we pray, we should present our requests in a humble and submissive spirit, and say, "O Lord, I would like this thing, or that, very much. I pray thee do it for me, but you know what is best both for me and for these about me, and I leave it to your judgment. Your will be done."

There are two kinds of prayer

(1) Prayer for objects which you know God is always willing to bestow, because he has said so in his Word. These things include such blessings as pardon, purity, peace, the Holy Spirit, and such temporal things as are necessary, and which he is glad for you to enjoy.

You can be quite sure that he is always willing to heal backslidings, give you a pure heart, baptize you with the Holy Spirit, etc., because you have his word for it.

(2) Then there are those other blessings which he makes his people know that he is willing to bestow by the direct revelation of the Holy Spirit in their hearts. God, by his Spirit, not only teaches us how to pray, but suggests the things for which we should ask. Paul explains this when he says, "The Spirit also helpeth our infirmities, for we know not what we should pray for as we ought, but the Spirit itself maketh intercession for us with groanings which cannot be uttered."

Doubtless Elijah had a direct revelation from God in his heart of the drought that was coming on Israel. How else could he have said to the king, "As the Lord God of Israel liveth, there shall not be dew nor rain in Israel except according to my word?"

He did not get that from the Scriptures nor from the holy men about him. No! the voice of the Lord spoke it direct in his heart.

Just so the same voice made plain to him on Mount Carmel that God was willing to send rain. Elijah believed and prayed, and the rain came.

When God makes you understand that your possession of any particular blessing is in harmony with his will, and that it may be had on condition of your prayer and faith, then you are not called upon to say "If it be they will," because you know already that it is just what he wishes. It is thus your privilege or duty to ask, to wrestle and believe until you receive it.

But there are many things that seem very desirable to us, of which we are in ignorance at the time we desire them as to whether it will be better or worse for us to have them. I have named several, and when we come to ask them from God I think we should do so with all submission to him, and subject to their bestowment appearing to be good and desirable in his sight.

7. I now come to consider one of the most important parts of successful prayer, if not the most important of all, and that is "faith." I say important, because the Bible says that "without faith it is impossible to please God," and over and over again, in one form or another, it declares that "according to our faith it shall be done unto us." You will remember that God in that wonderful eleventh chapter of Hebrews says, "He that cometh to God must believe that he is, and that he is a rewarder"—that is, an answerer of prayer—"of all those who diligently seek him." Now, the first thing you have to do is to believe. But you say, "What must I believe?" Well:

1. First, you must believe that God hears you when you pray. I spoke of that in my first letter. I need not go over it again. But you will not make any progress on my ladder unless you can realize yourself that you are really talking to God.

2. Then, secondly, you must believe that God understands your prayer, knows what you want, and how best to deal with it. I read the other day

about a little boy of six years, whose mother had been sick with small-pox, and taken from home to the hospital. The child could not understand how his mother could love him and yet leave him, so he decided to write a letter and ask her. Accordingly, he got a sheet of paper and scrawled all over it, and then he got an envelope and put his letter in and scrawled on that. Then he gave it to his father, who told him that no living creature could read it. However, he sent it to the child's mother, who laughed and cried when she saw it, saying that she could read every word of it. She then wrote him an answer, and told him just what he wanted to know.

It will be so with your prayers. Nobody on earth may be able to understand them, you may hardly understand them yourself, but your Father will know all about them, and send you the answer that you need.

3. You must believe that your Father will answer your prayer, that is, if he sees that what you ask will be best for you. You would not like him to give you what he saw was not good for you, however earnestly you might seek it. Neither would you like him to grant you your request if he foresaw that such response would prove injurious to those about you. But you must believe that, if he can do so in harmony with his holy will, he will give you what you ask. Indeed he may answer your request by giving you something much better for you and yours than the thing you have asked for.

If you pray for blessings promised to you then and there on the simple condition of believing prayer, believe that the answer comes while you wait. For instance, if you have grieved him and are conscious that you sincerely repent, believe that he forgives you on the spot.

If you want more of the Holy Spirit's light and love and joy, remember how eager God is to give it, and believe that your Father bestows it on you while bowed before him. He will surely do it.

If you want the sanctifying power, ask for it this very moment, believe that he answers your prayer, whether you have any inward evidence or no. He will give you the assurance in due time.

15

Prayer—Why Pray?

SOME PEOPLE EXPERIENCE MUCH difficulty as to the reason for prayer. They do not see why God cannot give them all the things they need in order to have life and health and godliness without having to ask for them. "Why," they ask, "should God require us to pray before he will help us?"

To that question I reply that God has certainly not appointed prayer in order to obtain information as to the character and extent of our needs, for, as we have seen, he knows them already far better than we know them ourselves.

Neither does he tell us to pray in order that we may instruct him how to help us. Alas! we often have to confess ourselves utterly unable to see in what form deliverance can come, and so have to throw ourselves on his wisdom.

Neither does he want us to pray in order to create a willingness in him to help us. He is more eager to deliver us out of the hands of our enemies and bless us with all needed good than we are to receive those gifts. Why, then, does he call us to seek them "with all prayer," to "pray without ceasing"—to pray after the fashion that the widow entreated the unjust judge—that is, to let God have no rest until he answers our requests. What can be the reason for all this?

I

1. The first reason I give why we should pray is the simple fact that God has willed that it should be so. Of his own wisdom he has decreed that prayer should be a means whereby his blessings should be poured into our hearts and lives and homes.

If you were to ask why some people are sick and others well, why some live and others die, why men walk on the earth instead of flying in the air, the only answer that could be found would be because under the circumstances God has willed it that it should be so, and our duty is to accept and conform ourselves to the arrangement, whether we see the reason for doing so or not. We are to walk by faith, and not by sight.

2. Another reason why we should pray, which is closely allied to the last one, is to be found in the fact that God has made all our mercies to depend on the use of means of one kind or the other, and one of the means he has appointed is prayer.

He says, "Ask, and it shall be given you; seek, and ye shall find; knock, and it shall be opened unto you." Again he says, "I will that men pray everywhere." But I may almost say that the Bible is full of passages which show that God has made prayer to be the means by which he has chosen to pour down the blessings of his grace into men's hearts and lives. You see this principle at work all through the world of nature. All God's creatures, so far as we know them, have to use means in order to their maintenance in health and well-being. The bird must fly and the fish must swim, the animal must hunt and the man must toil in order to eat and live.

Just so with the spiritual world. Men and women must use the means God has chosen in order to attain and keep and enjoy peace and purity and joy on earth, and finally to enter heaven. One of the most important of the different means ordained for that purpose is prayer.

It would be as sensible for a man to ask why he should work for his daily bread, when God could have arranged for his·wants being supplied without the labor of his hands, as to ask why he should pray when God could have met his needs without his being troubled to ask God to supply them.

But here the question may be asked, "Do not a great many blessings come to us irrespective of the offering of any prayers for them? In other words, can I not have good things without their being prayed for?" I reply, "I am not sure that they do. On the contrary, I think that it is very probable that every good thing we enjoy or ever shall enjoy comes in answer to somebody's prayer. Indeed, I shall not be surprised to find in the next world that not a single blessing comes to man which has not been prayed for by someone." But here a comrade may say, "Nobody ever prayed for me." That is a serious mistake, my friend, a multitude of prayers have gone up to heaven for us all. For instance:

1. Jesus Christ prayed for you when he cried out upon the cross, "Father, forgive them for they know not what they do," and we were especially referred to when, just before the agony of Gethsemane, he prayed, "Neither pray I for these alone, but for them also which shall believe on me through their word." You are one of those who have believed on him, my comrade, and can therefore say, "Jesus prayed for me."

Indeed, the Savior is praying for you on his intercessory throne while you are reading this letter. For the Bible tells us that "he ever liveth to make intercession for us." As the dear old song says:

> Arise, my soul, arise,
>> Shake off thy guilty fears,
> The bleeding Sacrifice
>> On my behalf appears
> Before the throne my Surety stands,
>> My name is written on his hands.

> He ever lives above,
>> For me to intercede,
> His all-redeeming love,
>> His precious blood, to plead,
> His blood atoned for all our race,
>> And sprinkles now the throne of grace.

> Five bleeding wounds he bears,
>> Received on Calvary,
> They pour effectual prayers.
>> They strongly plead for me.
> "Forgive him, oh, forgive!" they cry,
>> "Nor let that ransomed sinner die!"

Don't you think that God takes notice of the prayers of his dear Son, and in answer to them sends blessings down upon us all? I do.

2. Then, again, don't you think blessings come to us through the prayers that were offered for us by the saints who are now in glory.

and by our kindred who anxiously and lovingly prayed for us before we could pray for ourselves.

Have not many of us been blessed with fathers and mothers who have prayed for us? I have no doubt that my dear mother offered thousands of prayers for me, and I am sure that my dear wife wrestled in prayer for our children from the hour of their birth until her voice was lost in death.

Do all these prayers go unanswered? Oh, dear, no!

3. Then, again, I am sure that blessings come to us Salvationists in response to the prayers of our comrades all round the world. I wonder how many prayers are offered for me every day of my life. I shall never forget an old man coming to the window of my railway car while on a long journey across the lonely veldt in the heart of South Africa, far from any town or city, and saying, "General, I don't belong to your people, but I pray for you every day of my life."

Don't you pray for your comrades? You ought to do. They pray for you, and many of the blessings you enjoy doubtless come in answer to their prayers.

4. But perhaps you say, "Do these remarks apply to unconverted people?" Yes, of course they do, for beyond question they get prayed for. Jesus Christ said that his disciples were "the salt of the earth. That is, they keep it from corruption and decay and death. They hold back the last great fires that will burn it up, and thus they prevent many of its inhabitants being cast into hell. They do this by their example and their labors, and especially by their prayers.

5. Then, don't you think that the prayers you offer yourselves have some influence with God? I do. Don't you remember how night after night when you were but little children, innocent of the evils that in after days came into your hearts, you asked God to make you good, and take you to heaven when you die, and have you not been praying for yourselves for years since then?

To me it seems that all these prayers go up before God and are registered in his Book. If there is a remembrance book for your sins, I am sure there is a remembrance book for your prayers. And all the prayers that Jesus Christ, and your fathers and mothers, and your comrades, have offered for you, and all the prayers that have gone up from your own hearts, are registered in that book of intercession.

I am afraid that many people think very little of their prayers either before, at the time, or after they are offered, and yet, you may take it from me, my comrades, that God sets great store by your prayers, and that "praying breath is never spent in vain." He says, "The prayers of the righteous avail much," and he answers them, if not in the way they desire, in the best way that he possibly can.

So, seeing that your prayers bring answers down, and that you have yourselves reaped so rich a harvest in return from your own and other people's praying, keep on pleading with God, and he will assuredly keep on answering as long as you pray.

II

A little thought will enable us to discover other reasons why God has made prayer a means by which we can get the help he sees we need, and he can impart the assistance he desires to give.

1. Prayer is useful because calculated to impress the soul with a sense of its own dependence on God.

One of the dangers to which we are constantly exposed in this life is that of forgetting God, that is, of living, and working, and even going through a form of religious work, as though there is no God.

Now, one of the first things prayer does is to make us realize the actual existence of God, and to feel our dependence on him. That realization is a great help and blessing in our lives.

2. Then, prayer is favorable to the exercise of all those duties which have to do with our own peace and holiness and the salvation of those around u.

When a soldier prays that God will keep him safe, and supply his needs, and save his family, and make him successful in winning souls, the questions must come up in his heart: "Am I doing what I can to bring these things about? Am I resisting temptation, living consistently, and doing all I can for those I desire to be saved?" And as it must be a good thing to be urged forward in the discharge of such duties, it must be a good thing to pray.

3. Again, prayer is calculated to lead us to value at their true worth the blessings prayed for when they are received. It must be a reason-

able thing that we should set some store by the blessings he gives us. That which costs us nothing is often little prized, but when we have had a hard struggle, or paid a heavy price for a thing, we are likely to set some store by it, and to make the best use we can of it. Does not this rule apply to prayer?

4. Prayer promotes a sense of gratitude in the soul for the blessings received. What we have earnestly sought for with great desire and persevering faith, we are very likely to feel truly thankful to God for giving to us when we receive it, and grateful people are generally happy people.

5. By prayer we have a share in the reward that comes through God working by us.

6. God has ordained that we shall pray, because prayer affords the most convenient opportunity, and is the easiest method of communion with himself. He wants to come into the closest association with his people. He finds pleasure in fellowship with holy men and women. He has always been striving to meet with man from the days of Adam, Enoch, Abraham and Moses. The Lord Jesus Christ manifested the same desire when he was here on the earth. Genuine prayer includes all the elements of this communion, or as we sometimes call it, "fellowship" with God.

Communion with God is precious. You can never find out how really valuable it is till you experience it for yourself.

It is useful. Nothing so quickly sharpens men's minds, and cultivates their powers of heart and will as fellowship with God. It does for a man what the sun does for the corn.

It is delightful! There is no happiness greater than being in the company of those we most love, and it is just so with God, if we love him, communion with him will be delightful to us.

To commune with nature, with all her wonders of flowers, trees, mountains, rivers and seas, with her living creatures, the beautiful animals that roam over the earth, the sweet singing birds that fill the air with their praise—that is a great delight.

To commune with men—men of mind and thought, who have searched out the mysteries of things, to commune with holy men—men who are like God, who live the life of humble prayer and faith, to commune with useful men—men who have done something to benefit their fellows, to make the world better and happier, that is a wonderful privilege, but in prayer we commune with the great God, we talk to him, we think about him, we feel with him, we sympathize with him, and rejoice in him who is nature's King and the great Maker of men.

Prayer is the easiest form of communion. It is possible to all men at all times, the doors of his temple are ever open, his eyes are ever looking for us to draw near, and his ear is ever open to our cry.

7. Prayer is appropriate to all seasons and all places. I remember hearing, many years ago, of a young chimney-sweep who got converted, but who had an infidel employer, who would not let him bring his religion into the house, and contrived to prevent his having any place in which to pray. Those were the days in which the sweeps were obliged to climb up the chimneys in order to sweep them, and at last the dear lad found his place of prayer when he climbed up through the big chimney-pots. His employer could not reach him up there, and there was nothing between him and God's blue sky.

Well, you may not have to go up the chimney to pray, but remember that in any place you can pray, cry to God, and he will hear.

8. And it is one of the most beautiful things about prayer that it is good and proper under all circumstances. Indeed, the Savior said, "Men ought always to pray," and Paul told us to "pray without ceasing."

In health, never neglect to pray.

In sickness, prayer will be a consolation, it is a strength in suffering, a joy in pain.

When dying, prayer will bring the angels of God to your chamber, sustain and comfort those you leave behind, help you to triumph in the cold waters of Jordan, and bring you, in joy, to see your heavenly Father's face at last.

16

Unanswered Prayer

I FANCY THAT A great many comrades get puzzled and discouraged because they think that their prayers are not answered.

They say to themselves, I fear, and sometimes to those about them, "What is the good of my praying? Nothing seems to come of it." In this state of mind the devil finds it an easy task to persuade them to give up praying altogether, or to so take the heart out of their petitions that they become little more than the merest form.

Now, I want to look at this question of unanswered prayer, and see if I cannot find some explanation on the matter that will be helpful to those who may be perplexed with it. And in doing so I remark—

1. That there can be no question amongst us Salvationists that a great many prayers are answered—how many we shall never know. I tried to show you this in a former chapter. Real prayer cannot be offered without some response being made to it.

The Bible records are full of wonderful instances of prevailing prayer. I have already named some of them. They are so fascinating that I would like to go over them again, but my space will not allow. Read them for yourselves in your Bibles, and study and imitate the men and women who moved earth and heaven with their believing prayers.

The history of God's people since Bible days is crowded with miraculous manifestations that have come in answer to prayer.

The story of the Salvation Army is one long series of interventions by the Holy Spirit made in reply to earnest prayer.

But still, there do, doubtless, remain a great many petitions to which, so far as we can see, no reply is made from the throne of grace.

But here mistakes may easily be made. No doubt, many people conclude that their requests are not attended to because the reply comes in a different way from that they expected, or they don't come at the time named, or by giving something far more valuable than what was asked for.

Perhaps they asked for what their Father saw would be a stone, and so he gave them bread, or what he knew would prove a stinging scorpion, and he gave them a fish. So that, though in a different form from that for which they supplicated, their prayers were answered all the same.

2. But when all has been said and done, there can be no question but that a great deal of praying comes to nothing, or nearly so. It brings little, if any, blessing to man, and is taken little, if any, notice of by God.

Now, why is this? How is it that so many prayers go unanswered? Doubtless, there are many reasons.

I will mention three or four.

1. Many prayers go unanswered because they are so heartless.

You can't make prayer—real prayer, without heart. You can do business and earn money, write books and fight battles, and dance and sing, and do many other things without feelings, but you cannot offer the prayer which moves the heart of God and brings salvation down without putting heart into it yourselves.

The mere going through a form of words may pass with men, and even satisfy your own poor sleepy conscience, but it won't pass muster at the court of heaven, and if your praying has been of this character no wonder that no answer has come in response to it.

I remember hearing of an old man who got converted when he was seventy-three. He had learned a prayer when he was three years of age, and after he was saved and began to pray in reality, he said, "I am the old man who has been saying his prayers for seventy years, but never prayed all the time."

Multitudes of people say multitudes of prayers, but they never pray in reality, and, consequently, what they call their prayers go unnoticed by God.

2. Many petitions are not answered because there is something opposed to the spirit of their prayers in the lives of those who offer them.

David speaks out plainly on this matter. He says, "If I regard iniquity in my heart the Lord will not hear me." It was not "If I get drunk, or blaspheme, or go into some flagrant sin," but "If I tolerate evil desires or feelings in my heart, the Lord will neither hear nor answer my prayer."

Paul says, "I will therefore that men pray everywhere, lifting up holy hands, without wrath and doubting." That was Paul's wish, or rather, the wish of the Holy Spirit speaking through Paul. He wills that anywhere and everywhere you should lift up your hands to God, but they must not be soiled with blood, or trickery, or lust, or sin of any kind.

Let your hearts cry out to him, but there must be no unjust or cruel anger, or blind unbelief, or bad feelings in them. God is waiting for you, always willing to hear and bless, more willing to give than you to receive, but if your hands are impure and your hearts are cursed with envy or unbelief, don't expect him to answer or to bless you.

3. Many prayers go unanswered because the people who offer them are unwilling to take their own share in the work.

A little boy at family prayers one morning heard his father, a rich man, asking the Lord to feed the poor. "Father," said the boy, "I wish I had all the corn you've got in the barn." "What for?" said the father. "Then," said the lad, "I would answer your prayer."

God can hardly be expected to feed the hungry, and heal the sick, and help the distressed, and save the wicked, when the people ask him, if they are too miserly or too lazy to do what they can to accomplish the work themselves. In reply to such requests I think he would be likely to say, "Answer your own prayers. When you are prepared to do what you can in that direction I will help you."

4. The reason a great many prayers are not answered is simply want of faith. Nobody would be more surprised than a great many people would be if God did answer their petitions.

You have heard of the old lady who was much troubled by a mountain that towered up at the back of her cottage. It blocked out her view of the surrounding county and was otherwise inconvenient. One night she read in her text what Jesus Christ said about faith even as small as a grain of mustard seed removing a mountain, so she knelt down and prayed "O Lord, I want you to remove the mountain at the back of my house, O Lord, I do believe that you do remove it! I do believe that you do." Then she said, "Now we shall see!"

The next morning she called her son Tom to take down the shutter, and see if the mountain was gone. Tom took down the shutter. "Is it there?" she called out. "Yes, mother, the mountain is there," he replied. "Ah, yes," said the old lady, "I thought it would be. It is just what I expected." So much for her faith. Now, if, as we have quoted over and over again in this chapter, our prayers are answered according to our faith, where there is no faith we have no ground to expect an answer.

5. My paper is full, and yet there is one of the most common reasons of all for unanswered prayer yet to notice, and that is "impatience."

This is a hurrying, scurrying age. Everybody wants to do big things of all kinds, and among the rest they want Jehovah to do wonders for them. They would like him to heal their bodies, to deliver them in their trials, to purify their hearts, to baptize them with the Holy Ghost, to save their families and crowds of sinners, and ever so many other things. They ask God to do these things for them, but they have not time to properly make their requests, and less time still to wait for the great God to answer. So that if he does not respond to their prayers right away the whole thing is passed over, except that they dare to complain that God does not answer prayer.

And now I have nothing more to say to you at present on the subject of prayer. My last word is: Pray on, pray always, pray without ceasing. And among those you pray for most earnestly and most constantly, I would ask you ever to remember your general.

17

The Doing of Difficult Duties

THE SUBJECT IS IMPORTANT because it is so closely connected with your peace of mind. Duty neglected plants a thorn in the conscience which spoils the soul's quietness. It has to do with the favor of God, for he cannot smile upon his children when neglecting their duty. In short, duty has to do with the honor of your Master, the salvation of souls, the happiness of a dying hour, and the "Well done" of the Judgment Day. All will agree therefore, I am sure, that doing your duty is a most important matter.

But important as the subject is, everyone will know that the more important duties of life seldom present themselves to us without the company of some difficulty or other. There is usually something which comes with them, or follows after them, which makes their discharge unpleasant, or painful, and sometimes even perilous to life itself.

Out of these difficulties all sorts of excuses are made for the neglect of duty, and often constitute the reasons why the duties are left undone. Therefore, I want to encourage you with all my might in the doing of your duty, by a few considerations which I hope you will seriously ponder, and my first piece of advice is:

1.Be careful to satisfy yourself, as far as you can, that the work to which you are urged is your duty. The devil can manufacture sham duties, anyway he can tempt people to the following of evil courses, by labelling them as duties. Jesus Christ told his apostles that the time was coming when those who murdered them would think they were thereby rendering God service. That is, the devil would try to persuade these people that in killing Christ's disciples they were doing their duty.

Beware of this device of Satan, and beware also of making yourself unhappy about doing work which, however practical and desirable for others, is neither practical nor desirable for you, and therefore is not your duty. It may be the duty of your captain, or your sergeant-major, or of some comrade who is wiser and more experienced than you are, or of some comrade who has been appointed to do it, but it may not be your duty, and therefore not required of you. Anyway not at present. When you are wiser and stronger, it may come to your turn, and you will then be able to deal with it.

2. If, however, you are satisfied that any particular work is your duty you must give yourself up to the doing of it, whatever difficulties may seem to block the way. Duty is duty—and no difficulties, great or small, no dangers, big or little, no enemies, many or few, can excuse you from the doing of it.

Consequences cannot affect your obligation. You can only serve God, follow Christ, save souls, and find your way to Heaven by bearing your cross, and that means doing your duty, in the face of difficulty, danger and death. Christ did not shrink from duty because Calvary barred his way. His flesh cried out before all Heaven and earth and hell, in dark Gethsemane and on the cruel cross, that the road he had to travel was a difficult one, but he did not abandon his task on that account. No, he went on, and paid the price of your redemption and mine with his precious blood. He did his duty.

But you can always remember that many of the seeming difficulties in the way of doing your duty are only things of the imagination, things that will vanish away at close quarters. Indeed, where the duty is boldly undertaken they will be often found to be blessings in disguise.

We all know that a great many people refuse to look at religion because they think it requires from them duties which they imagine will be disagreeable, indeed which they think they could never bring themselves to discharge, and we all know also that when these same people do embrace it and give themselves up to the duties it requires, that they very often cry out, "Oh how delightful! I did not know that loving and serving God and fighting for the salvation of my neighbors and friends was anything like so blessed a work as this. Why, I am happier a thousand times in doing this duty than ever I was in neglecting it."

The same argument applies to going forth as an officer, speaking in the open-air, playing in the band, praying in the family, selling the War Cry, honesty in our daily labor, and in almost every other duty in connection with life and godliness. Looked at from a distance they often seem difficult, but when undertaken the difficulty proves to have had no real existence.

3. It must be also borne in mind that where the difficulty in the discharge of any duty is a reality, strength equal to the need is supplied at the time. When the difficulties connected with duty are looked at, it is only too common to leave God but of our calculations. We forget that he will be there to assist us in the doing of his will. He has promised that his grace shall be sufficient, and that as our day, so shall our strength be.

We have all heard the story of the negro who said if God told him to jump through the stone wall, it was his duty to jump and God's business to see he went through. Now, if you go for your duty, however difficult it may appear, God will see that you have grace to go through with it.

4. We should also bear in mind that in many cases the difficulties connected with the doing of the duty arise from the indecision felt with respect to it. While halting between two opinions with respect to any action, walls of impossibility rise up before us, but when a decision has been reached the walls vanish or the soul bounds over them with all the ease and fleetness of a deer leaping over a mountain brook.

How often we have seen this exemplified in the anxious soul struggling with anguish while weighing up the difficulties involved in a salvation life. While undecided, the penitent-form appears just impossible, but when the mind is made up for God and eternal life, the mercy-seat has been faced without an atom of difficulty.

5. Then, my comrades, you must not forget how wonderfully God delights to honor the men and the women who boldly enter the path of duty in the face of difficulty. The Bible is full of stories regarding the glorious triumphs of men and women of like passions with ourselves, men and women who have triumphed over suffering and death and devils while discharging their God-given duty. And the more striking the difficulties they have had to encounter the more remarkable have been the victories they have gained.

As a most wonderful illustration of my subject look again at those three Hebrew lads who dared to do their duty in the face of the wrath of the mightiest monarch of their day. The furnace was roaring like thunder, the heat coming forth in sulphurous waves, penetrating even the very court in which the monarch sat. His countenance was full of fury. He stormed and raved like one gone mad. That these three boys should set him and all his powers at naught was more than he could have supposed possible, and infuriated him beyond measure. "Talk not to me of your duty to your God," said he: "Who is he? Where is he? What can he do? You shall bow to my authority and do my will, or you shall be burnt to ashes. I will give you time to consider."

"We require no time for consideration," they answered meekly, but firmly. "The power to burn, oh, wicked king, is yours, unless our God interferes, but the duty to refuse your commands is ours, and let it be known unto you, O mighty monarch, that if we burn we will not bow." They did their duty, and God saw to it that they did not burn.

18

Contentment with Small Efforts

Doing the Same Thing Over Again

1. THE OBLIGATION OF doing something real and effective for his Savior, and the salvation of his fellows, is continually being urged upon every soldier in the Army. The Bible insists upon it. The captain urges it. The Holy Spirit calls for it. Jesus Christ commands it. The death angel suggests it.

> *Go, labor in my vineyard,*
> *You'll receive a sure reward,*
> *You'll hear the inward whisper,*
> *It is your dying Lord.*

2. This obligation to engage in the Salvation fight is generally admitted amongst us. No one reading this will deny this duty. Every soldier says to himself every day he lives in almost every prayer he offers, every song he sings, every address he hears—anyway every time he attends a meeting where the power of God is felt: "Yes, I ought to live and fight for souls." "I ought to do something in response to all my Savior's love and sacrifice for me."

3. Many of my dear soldiers not only admit that this is their duty, but make strong and constant efforts to discharge it. They rise early and sit up late in order to find time to roll the old chariot along. They sacrifice their home joys and outdoor recreations, and shorten their hours of labor to stand by the open-air, bombard the drink-shops, teach the juniors, or engage in some other department of the War.

They give all the money they can spare from their hard earnings, and often deny themselves of little luxuries and comforts to support the work.

They wrestle and pray, and hope and believe, and find the chief satisfaction of their lives in the prosperity of their corps and the conversion of sinners.

4. But over against all this beautiful devotion and love, which no one can possibly admire more than does their General, we have, I fear, a rather numerous class of soldiers who try to satisfy their consciences on this subject by putting forth only the feeblest efforts and the realization of the smallest results.

Their ambition is low. Indeed, they can scarcely be said to aim at anything in particular in the little they do attempt. Their expectation is trifling.

Then, what they do one day they are content to do the next. They go through the same forms, sing the same songs, offer the same prayers, give the same testimonies, tell the same anecdotes, quote the same texts, and are satisfied with seeing the same result, and only too often without seeing any results at all.

Round and round and round again they go with the same things, although at every turn they see the world struggling with restless efforts to gain its godless, selfish ends, and the devil seeking to damn their families, neighbors and friends with devices ever new.

Now, this contentment with small and feeble things is, I think, much to be deplored, and that for many reasons.

The fighting loses its charm. Doing the same thing in the same way, and nothing, or but little, coming of it, sickens the soldiers of their own efforts, and makes everybody about them sick of them too.

Sinners are hardened by the powerless repetitions of the means employed to save them.

Backsliders are manufactured.

Officers lose heart by the lack of interest in the meetings.

Infidels triumph over the powerlessness of the means used for the salvation of men.

The children grow up counting religion a feeble, uninteresting thing and, generally speaking, the devil triumphs, and the world asks the question, "Where is the God that is so much boasted about?"

What is the remedy? This is a soldier's question. This is your affair. No one will deny the assertion that if the individual soldiers of the Army could all be fired up with the spirit of earnestness, and love, and zeal, that they could change the face of the world, and roll back the mighty stream of redeemed souls that is now coursing its way to everlasting woe.

But what is the soldier who knows that he belongs to this half-asleep class of which I have been referring, to do to rescue himself? I answer:

Look at what you are doing for God fairly and squarely in the face and honestly answer the following questions about it:

(a) How does your work look when measured by your own convictions of what is your duty? Are you doing as much for God and souls as you feel you ought, and are you doing it as faithfully and as effectually as you can?

(b) How does your work look when measured by the need of the dying sinners in your own home, neighborhood, or the big world about you?

(c) How do you think your work will appear in your eyes when you look at it in the light of the great White Throne? What sort of an opinion will you form of your praying and singing and talking when they are all laid bare before the gaze of God, angels, and men? Will they be seen on that great day to be as earnest and as real and as thorough as they ought to have been? Shall you think so yourself?

(d) How does your work appear to you when compared with what some of your comrades have done or are doing? Do not the energy and sacrifice and faith of these dear soldiers shame you, and make you blush to think how contented you are with your cold, heartless way of going through your duties?

(e) How does your work of today compare with the work you did yourself in the days gone by? Are you as much in earnest and as punctual and as compassionate as you were then?

(f) How does your work and the way you do it look when you remember what your dear Savior did for you?

Oh, my comrades, if on honestly looking into your hearts and at your work you find room for dissatisfaction, start at once to try and mend matters, and begin by doing something you have never done before this very day. Anyway, start off by throwing your soul with all the earnestness you can muster into what you do attempt. Oh, do, do make a big fight to get out of this jogtrot, cold, heartless manner of doing things!

Make a new consecration of all you have and are to the service of your Lord. Have a definite transaction with him, and make up your mind to be a soulwinner whatever may come. I was once down in the rut of contentment with the mere form of doing things, but I broke away and got deliverance. How it came about I will tell you next week, all well. But don't wait till then before you definitely start to make the very most of yourself in this fight for God and the souls of men.

—PART THREE—
THE MARKETPLACE

19

Wasted Time

I WANT TO BRING before you a topic not often discussed, and yet of vast importance. I mean the use you make of your time.

We hear a good deal about wasted money, and not a bit too much. There is a crying need for more warning and instruction on that subject, for there never was a period of such scandalous wastefulness as the present. But we do not hear much about wasted time. And yet time, if rightly employed, will bring money and every other blessing we need, both for this world and the world to come.

By time, you will know that I mean the moments, and hours, and days, that are now passing over us.

What is time? A river flowing
To eternity's wide sea,
Forward whither all are going,
On its bosom bearing thee.

What is life? A bubble floating
On that silent, rapid stream,
Few, too few, its progress noting,
Till it bursts and ends the dream.

What a priceless treasure is time! What a value we ought to set by it! We profess to value things by what they will gain for us, or give us the opportunity of gaining. Not only does time afford the opportunity for benefiting others, or of benefiting ourselves, but all other agencies are useless without it. Means, and friends, and comrades are powerless to bless when time has come to an end.

1. Time gives the opportunity of personal salvation. "Now is the

accepted time, and now is the day of salvation." There is not a passage in the Bible that points to any safe ground for expecting deliverance from the penalty and pollution of sin in the world to come. It is now or never. We must be saved in time, there will be no chance in eternity.

It is in time that the heart can be purified. It was on the earth that the bloodwashed multitudes whom John saw washed their robes and made them white in the blood of the Lamb, and were thereby enabled to sing the praises of their Redeemer in heaven.

2. Time is precious because it affords the opportunity for personal improvement. Time is short. Short indeed, but it is long enough for the accomplishment of a remarkable amount of profitable work if we will but seize the moments as they fly and use them to good account.

It is surprising, for example, what wonders have been accomplished by men and women during the odd minutes of life. Valuable books have been written, difficult languages learned, important scientific discoveries made, curious and valuable works of art produced—indeed, all kinds of knowledge have been acquired by the use of those fragments of time that are ordinarily neglected or allowed to glide away unnoticed and unimproved.

I know that the lives of many of my dear soldiers are much occupied with the demands of their daily toil, or the unavoidable anxieties connected with their families. But still if they would but follow the examples I have named, they might redeem the needed time for a considerable amount of reading and thinking, and praying, and writing, each or all of which would help to qualify them for greater influence in the Salvation War. Try, my comrades, try!

3. Time provides the opportunity for saving our families, neighbors and friends. For this we admit our responsibility, and are in earnest to discharge it. If we do not pull them out of the fire of sin and land their feet on the narrow path, who will? We know that the cords of affection that bind us together give us great influence with each other. We want to use it in the right direction of righteousness, and we know that now is our only chance of discharging this important duty.

Oh! you fathers and mothers, sons and daughters, brothers and sisters, the word "now!" ought to be ever ringing in your ears. Now is your only chance for gaining your end.

4. It is only in time that we can help our dear Savior to complete his redeeming work. Perhaps we shall be able to do something in the direction of rescuing the perishing in the world to come. I don't know! But I do know that it is here that Jesus Christ most sorely needs our help. There will be co-workers in abundance in the skies. It is in this life that he is short of willing hands, scheming brains and burning hearts. Won't you use your time to help him?

5. It is in time that we can lay up treasure in heaven. I don't pretend to understand all about it, but I do think that the Bible teaches that it is in time that we determine the kind of people we shall be in eternity. I don't mean merely that it is down here that we settle whether we shall spend eternity in heaven or in hell, but what our character and lot will be in whichever world we shall enter when we die.

You who read this are going to heaven. I assume it. You say so. I believe you. But the kind of people you will be when you get there, the measure of the happiness you will enjoy, the hold you will have on your Heavenly Father's heart, the position of honor you will occupy, the character of the mansion you will inhabit, and the amount of blessedness you will enjoy, will all depend on the way you spend your days down here—that is, on the way you occupy your time.

You may be careless and self-indulgent in the use you make of your time, and yet, perhaps, by the mercy of God, get into heaven at last, but if you do, the heaven you will reach will be a very poor and unsatisfactory affair compared with what it would have been had you resolutely and self-sacrificingly redeemed and employed your time for God and souls.

What importance, O my comrades, do these considerations give to the way in which you are spending your time? It is rapidly passing away.

> *Our life as a dream,*
> *Our time as a stream*
> *Glides swiftly away,*
> *And the fugitive moment refuses to stay.*

The loss of time is irreparable, it cannot be regained. It is like water spilt upon the ground which cannot be gathered up again. And yet how little we think of its value until it is gone. A celebrated poet says:

"We take no thought of time but from its loss,
To give it, then, a tongue is wise in man."

But would it not be better to let our days and hours talk to us as they fly, and to turn them to good account while yet they are ours, than simply to wail over them when they are flown, like the woman who, refusing to be comforted, cried out in her despair: "Call back my wasted time if you can, call back the time I have thrown away, then may there be some hope for me. But my time is gone."

Queen Elizabeth is reported to have cried out when dying, "A million of money for a moment of time." Reclining on her royal couch, surrounded by the choicest luxuries the world could produce, the head of one of the greatest kingdoms on the earth, she craved a few fragments of the time she had thoughtlessly wasted during her life, for the all-important task of preparing for eternity. But all the kingdoms of the earth could not purchase the coveted moment of time. Her hour had come, and for her the angel's proclamation had gone forth, that "time should be no more!"

O my comrades, are you satisfied with the use you are making of your precious minutes as they pass you by? There is an old story of some prisoner who was informed that the whole of his water supply was placed in a large cistern at the top of his cell, out of his sight and beyond his reach. When that was exhausted he was told that no more would be given him, and that consequently he would have to die. Now you can readily imagine how carefully that prisoner would use that water. Every drop would be precious because he could not know whether it might not be his last.

Comrades, the measure of time given us on earth is equally unknown to us. This may be our last year, our last month, our last day, our last night. Let us use it wisely and truly, and bravely, for the highest welfare of ourselves, the benefit of our fellows and the glory of our King.

20

About Clothes

MAN HAS BEEN DESCRIBED as a clothes-wearing animal. It cannot be said that he is the only animal that wears clothes, because there are few of the creatures that walk the earth around him, or dwell in the sea beneath him, or fly in the air above him, that are not as usefully and as becomingly clothed as he is—most of them much more so. Still, he is the only creature on this planet who has any power of choice or change in the character of his outer covering, or in the matter of putting it on or taking off, which things I suppose go together to constitute a clothes-wearer in the sense that other animals are not.

Clothes may be put down as an absolute necessity from their all but universal use. There are few even of the tribes counted most barbarous that don't affect some kind of apparel, however simple and crude it may be, the purpose served by it being of the most varied character. To begin with:

1. Clothes may be regarded as a mark of civilization. To discover a race of people in any part of the globe who did not wear clothes would prove at once their savage state, pure and simple. One of the first things that the converts to civilization or Christianity do, in the forests of Africa, or in the jungles of India, is to get at once into some form of dress or other. Some soon come to measure the height to which their fellows have risen in the scale of civilization by the quantity and costliness, and often the ridiculous fashion, of the clothes they are able to bear about them.

Promote Decency

2. Clothes safeguard and promote proper feelings of decency. They are essential to chastity in the present condition of human nature. Of course, they can be so made, and so worn as to have an opposite effect,

such being, I am sorry to say, a too common course of things, the tendency of a good deal of dressing in these days being beyond question strongly in that direction. A great many of the fashions that prevail in what is known as the best society appear more lewd and suggestive of indecent thoughts and feelings than the semi-nudity of the old races that range the trackless forests of Darkest Africa, or of the lower castes in the cities and villages of India.

Whether clothes were worn before the fall or not is a controverted question. I am strongly inclined to think that they were, but there can be no question that if they were not instituted before the fall, they became a necessity for the maintenance of right and pure feelings immediately afterwards, and as to their usefulness in that direction there can be no question.

3. Clothes serve as a protection from those changes in the weather so unfavorable to the health and vigor of man which are found in every land. The animals, as a rule, are made for one climate only, hence one kind of dress serves their purpose with the little variation required by the changes of the seasons. But man has to live and labor in every clime, and consequently needs many changes of covering. If he is to live in any reasonable comfort, at one time under the burning suns of the tropics, at another on the fringes of the North Pole, and at another midway between them both, he must be able to change and adapt his outer garments to each.

Mark Social Distinctions

4. Clothes are useful as marking out social distinctions. There are differences in the positions, duties, and powers of mankind. One will be the master, and another the servant, one will be the governor, and another the governed, one will be rich, and the other poor. Some may, and will, object to these differences, and argue that all men ought to be on one level. But at present it is not so. It is, as we have said, the reverse, and no plans have as yet been contrived that will make it otherwise, and society being constituted with these distinctions, it is quite as well, nay, very desirable, that we should, with the least possible trouble, be able to discover what the position and conditions of those around us are. Clothes are very useful in this direction, indeed, the fact of their having been so

universally employed for the purpose reveals their utility. They serve:

(a) To mark out the caste or position of individuals. You can guess whether the man you meet on the street, or talk to in the hall, is rich or poor, educated or ignorant, by his clothes. Of course, you cannot be certain, but you can go a long way in the matter of supposition.

(b) By their dress you can distinguish the servant from his master or from her mistress. Clothes serve to distinguish trades and professions, and to mark out and give increased importance to authority. You do not want anyone to tell you whether a man is a policeman, or a priest, or a soldier, or a sailor, and when you go into a court you need no friend or usher to tell you which is the counsel, or which is the judge. Their clothes give the information. Just so clothes mark out rank. Kings, queens, and the great people about their person or their courts are all dressed in some form indicative of their high position.

Now, Salvationists are clothes-wearers, indeed, we are great at clothes, inasmuch as we have a style of dress which we call uniform, all to ourselves—clothing which, in shape, and color, is all our own. This dress we reckon—and reckon, I think, correctly—saves us from certain serious evils, and serves several very useful purposes. For instance:

1. It is an open confession of our Salvationism. It is a public acknowledgment of our Lord, of our espousal of his cause, and of our willingness that all the world should know the fact.

2. It is an open declaration that the wearer has given up wrong-doing, has come out from the world, is determined to be out-and-out for God, and is resolved to live and die for the salvation of men.

3. It makes opportunities for usefulness. Those who love God will recognize the Salvationist by it, and be delighted to converse with him. Those who hate religion will tackle him, thus giving him the opportunity to preach salvation. In fact, to almost all classes of people the uniform makes an occasion for talking about God, righteousness, and eternity.

Can Be Perverted

But necessary and useful as the clothes-wearing habit may be, like all other things good and useful in themselves, it can be perverted, and made into an evil. This is just what has happened, and the material, shape, and general character of clothes have become sources of temptation—indeed, they can be counted as among the most fruitful causes of evil with which poor human nature has to battle.

For instance, clothes, more than all else, may be the means of fostering and feeding the pride and vanity of the human heart. Introduced on account of the sin of our first parents, and therefore to be regarded as marks of their disgrace, it is curious to contemplate the extent to which their posterity has come to glory in their shape.

It is not probable that when clothes became a necessity, it was intended that they should disfigure or be out of harmony with the human form. On the contrary, it perfectly natural to suppose the opposite, but that they should be made to foster the vanity, occupy the time, and involve the extravagant expenditure that have come to be the usage in the present day, could hardly have been imagined. Oh, the waste and misery caused by the rage to be as finely dressed as, or to outdo, those about us!

The Army uniform saves the wearer from these absurd and extravagant rivalries, and gives a good and modest appearance, at immeasurably less cost than fashionable worldly apparel.

Most important of all, the uniform is a preacher. It makes people think about God and godliness.

If it is right to preach salvation with the tongue, it must be right to preach it by the clothes. The Salvationist, by his dress, preaches salvation to every one who sees him.

21

Personal Cleanliness

IN THE CHAPTER DEVOTED to the consideration of home, I said something about the desirability of having a clean house, clean furniture, and, in fact, so far as possible, everything within and without it clean, but, although alluded to, there was not much said about a clean person. I must, therefore, make a remark or two on that side of the subject.

Some people do not attach very much importance to a clean body. They will polish their faces, and cover themselves with feathers and flowers, and falderals and jewelry, while their bodies are defiled from head to foot. Some Salvationists, I am sorry to say, are not perfect in this direction. Now, this should not be. The Apostle Paul is very definite on the subject, for he distinctly commands that while the heart is to be sprinkled from an evil conscience, the body is to be washed with pure water. (Hebrews 10:22)

Now, a clean body must mean a body that is made and kept clean—face and hands and head and feet, and every other part of the frame, purged, washed from every kind of dirt, and kept clean.

1. A clean body is promotive of health. Anatomists tell us that there are over 2,000,000 pores—that is, little openings in the human frame—to be kept open for the purpose of giving out the impurities of the blood. In addition, these pores are intended to drink in the atmosphere, which ought, therefore, to be kept as pure as possible. Now, if all, or a portion of these 2,000,000 little mouths are kept closed by dirt, it can readily be seen that damage of some kind or other will be suffered by the system generally.

2. A clean body is agreeable to those persons with whom you associate. Dirty faces, fingers, teeth, or any other exposed parts of the person are most distasteful to comrades, or people of proper notions on the subject, and as dirt usually manifests itself by a disagreeable odor, it will

reveal its presence to the nose when it does not to the eyes, creating in either case sensations of unpleasantness if not of disgust.

3. A clean body usually accompanies a pure mind. There will be any number of individuals who will have the former without the latter, that is they will be cleanliness itself from top to toe, but will neither prize nor possess, the pearl of greatest price—a clean heart. But although, as a quaint old preacher says, "God has some very dirty children," there will not be very many who will have purity within who will not instinctively seek to be pure without.

Cleanliness, in the sense in which I am using the term, is possible to all, or nearly all. I am aware that many who will read this will be earning their daily bread for themselves and their families, engaged at employments that will necessarily begrime their clothes and their persons, such as colliers, foundrymen, engineers, stokers, and the like. They cannot avoid a certain amount of dirt clinging to their hands, faces, and persons generally. But that which is daily accumulated might be correctly styled clean dirt, and with ordinary care such workmen can keep themselves as sweet and clean as their comrades who are called to labor under different conditions. Soap can be had in endless variety nowadays, and at low enough cost. Water also can be had in abundance, except in exceptional circumstances, such as away in some of the gold fields, the toil required is not very great, and can be furnished by the individual himself.

Everyone should have a good wash all over at least once every week. There is no difficulty about this. A tub large enough to sit down in can be had for a trifle, a kettle full of hot water—rain water is, of course much the better, but if not procurable, a little washing soda will go far to soften hard water—a flat piece of soap and a good-sized towel are all that are required for the process. It is not necessary to expose all the body at once. Begin by removing the upper garments, and washing the upper parts of the body, and then go on to the lower.

The same plan will, with two or three pails of water, give you a cold bath every morning in summer and tepid one in winter. If anyone wants to know what can be done in the way of cleanliness with a tub of warm water, let him go and see the colliers in the coal districts.

A lamp bath is very simple, and may be taken once a week at a trifling cost. It not only refreshes and invigorates the body, but serves admirably to promote the cleanliness I am advocating.

A Turkish bath now and then is very useful indeed for this purpose. They are common in all the principal towns, and may be had in the evening at a low price. But, for the promotion of cleanliness, a good lamp bath is just as useful, more economical, will occupy less time, and can be taken at the most convenient hour.

22

Conversation

IN MY DISCUSSION OF everyday religion, I cannot pass by the subject of conversation, occupying, as it does, so large a space in the intercourse, and having so much to do with the intelligence, comfort and religion of Salvationists in all their relations to each other.

Everybody know that by conversation I mean that interchange of thought and feeling which takes place, in words, on a subject between two or more individuals on matters which interest one or more of the parties. Conversation is a very important privilege, common, we may well imagine, to almost all beings endowed with life.

I
They Talk in Heaven

We know that the great Father in Heaven holds communion with the holy beings by whom he is surrounded, hence it is quite possible that he does this through the medium of some celestial language. The Bible contains many talks that God has had with his people, or with those who were once his people. They nearly all begin with: "Thus saith the Lord." The Bible also contains the answers which the people, in various forms made to the Lord. In the heavenly state we are told that saint and cherub bow before his face, and cry out in his ears: "Holy, holy, holy, is the Lord God Almighty!"

Then, we are sure that the angels converse with each other. What wonderful themes they have to talk about, and what wonderful knowledge they possess on those subjects! Among other topics, we can have no doubt that they talk about the inhabitants of this world, their sins and sorrows, and about all the efforts God makes for their salvation.

They Talk in Hell

The devils converse together in Hell. They talk over their infernal schemes, and tell to each other the progress they make in carrying them out. There is no lack of interesting matter for conversation there.

The brute creation around us have, beyond question, some means of interchanging their thoughts and wishes that answers to conversation.

If animals can reason—and no one who has any knowledge of the habits of the ant or the dog, the horse or the rat, and many other of the creatures familiar to us, will be disposed to deny it—if they are capable of disinterested affection, and affection that is something greater than instinct—indeed, far ahead of that of which many human beings seem to be capable in relation to their kindred and friends. If they have some faculty which answers to conscience, is it not fair to suppose that they can communicate their ideas and feelings to each other? But how inferior, after all, are the faculties by which they do this compared with those with which man is endowed!

Talk Without Speech

The ability to converse is developed in man very early. The mother commences by talking to her babe with her eyes, the tender touch of her fingers, or the gentle pressure to her breast. Then one by one the easy words creep in until the vocabulary of language follows, by which almost every thought, desire, or feeling possible to man can be spoken and explained.

Whether conversation, as I have suggested, is common to the creatures round about us or not, however, there can be no question about its being common to man. Every man who has ever lived, has, I should think, possessed the power of conversing with his fellows. Of course, while the language of the tongue is the ordinary means by which conversation is carried on, still, when that gift is denied some other means are found. For instance, with what remarkable rapidity and correctness the deaf and dumb can communicate with each other!

In all the public meetings which I have held in Stockholm, if I turned to the gallery in our beautiful temple there, I have seen a body of this unfortunate class, to whom one or two officers who can hear were repeating, by signs upon their fingers and faces, the words I was speaking, and the songs we were singing, from the platform.

Talk Abused

The gift of conversation may be, and I am afraid commonly is, much abused. It is abused by godless people. It is probable that the tongue has been a greater curse to the world than the sword. The apostle describes it as the untameable organ, and as being "set on fire of Hell." "So is the tongue among our members, that it defileth the whole body, and setteth on fire the course of nature, and it is set on fire of Hell. For every kind of beasts, and of birds, and of serpents, and of things in the sea, is tamed, and hath been tamed of mankind, but the tongue can no man tame, it is an unruly evil, full of deadly poison." (James 3:6,7,& 8)

II

Apart from the more dreadful evils that are hatched, nursed and prepared for action in the course of conversation, what a fearful amount of time and ability do we see wasted in the useless chatter of ordinary talk! You have only to listen for an hour to the chatter in a railway compartment, or at the tables of a restaurant, or on board a steamer, to be disgusted with the weakness, nay, the absolute silliness of the talk that goes on. Men and women who have had a decent education, and who are intelligent and thoughtful in the business, or in the management of their homes, will sit for hours and pour forth a torrent of words which contain scarcely a grain of sense, to say nothing about utility, in them.

Faulty Salvationists

And I am afraid that Salvationists are not faultless in this direction. Officers and soldiers who will labor in the open-air, on a platform, in visitation, and in every other conceivable way, allow the chances of benefiting their power in conversation, to pass away unimproved. Not only so, but they will sometimes absolutely turn them to bad account, and make them sources of evil, such as the letting down of the religious tone of those present, especially the young, by lightness and frivolity, the damaging of the character of the absent by slanderous statements, the discouragement of such as may have been praying and believing for richer spiritual gifts, and the grieving of the Holy Spirit generally.

These evils are often wrought

1. From want of thought. One is carried away by the example of another. There is no evil intentions, but the evil is done, nevertheless.

2. The wish to be funny, to make those present laugh, and to make them regard the speaker as being witty. Whatever advantages there may be in that conclusion, I must confess to be unable to see. But some Salvationists I know will treasure up every piece of nonsense they may read in the press, or hear, or imagine, and pour it out at the first meeting with comrades they may have, often, I am ashamed to say, regardless of the presence of the ungodly and the young.

3. Some of those to whom I am referring will be guilty of this trashy talk in order to appear knowing. They cannot let a topic pass without saying something about it, regardless as to whether the subject itself, or what they have to say upon it, is either intelligent, or useful. They should remember, and be influenced by, the ancient sage who, when asked why he did not take part in a question that was afloat, replied, "What was to the point I could not say, and what was not to the point I would not say."

That will make a good rule for us all. Let us resolve that if we cannot say anything which is promotive of the general good feeling, and of positive profit to the company, we will not say anything at all.

Advantages of Conversation

1. The amount of profit and pleasure which conversation can be made to promote, cannot be overstated. To begin with, it provides valuable employment for time which must otherwise be wasted. Only let anyone count up the number of hours spent, in a single year, in company with kindred and friends, or strangers, and which afford us the chance for a little talk, and they will be surprised at the total. Take them at only three hours per day, and you have over one thousand, which, divided by ten (about the working hours of an average Salvationist), gives you one hundred days, or over fourteen weeks. Think of all this period going to waste, and then consider how at least a valuable portion of it can be profitably and agreeably em-

ployed in doing good to the bodies and souls and circumstances of those around us by the persevering practice of a little conversation.

III

2. Then, it must be borne in mind that in conversation we have opportunities for usefulness that we cannot find elsewhere. It always seems to me that people will take more notice of—in fact, will better understand—many things that are said over the table, or in a quiet, personal talk, than they will that which is shouted at them from the platform. For one reason, the thing spoken of will often be discussed in a more natural and understandable manner. Moreover, there is the opportunity of asking for information on matters that they do not exactly understand. Then, the people spoken to will talk back again, and that will compel them to think, and so altogether there is the tendency to spread information on useful subjects.

Further, there are the children, who, if trained to listen, will be ready to receive instruction from what is said around them. My own children were eager listeners to the conversations at our table, and those which were ever taking place in our family.

Moreover, we are surrounded, in every direction, by crowds of people whose minds are full of all sorts of strange, crooked, and false notions about God and religious experience, the Army, and other important questions. I seldom or never come up alongside strangers and get into conversation with them, indeed, I seldom read the articles that are written about us in the newspapers, magazines, and elsewhere—and that by really capable people—but I find them full of blunders and misrepresentations. Now, what is to be done with these people? They will not come and see and hear for themselves, neither will they read our books. It appears to me, therefore, that our greatest chance with them lies in the direction of conversation. Talk to them, hear their difficulties about the Army, about conversion, about faith, tell them your own experience, and God will help you to pour light into their minds.

3. Another valuable feature in conversation is found in the fact that it very frequently combines pleasure with usefulness. What privilege of duty is there on earth, apart from communing with God, that is more enjoyable than intelligent and sympathetic conversation? A meaning-

less gossip about the most trivial things has its charm, but to talk about matters of interest, of value, in which you are conscious that you have imparted useful thoughts, inspired holy feelings, and been instructed and inspired in return, is of the nature of the joy of Heaven.

Oh, how well I remember, in the days gone by—going back to my early youth—the delights of this character that were mine! Precious hours were those! How thoughts burned, language flashed, hearts were drawn closer, and resolves for heroic, Christlike deeds were framed! How the hours flew by, and the time of parting ended the glorious feast! Such hours and opportunities have not been withheld from me down to my latest years, and will be my portion, I trust, till I change the important communion of the saints on earth, for the blissful fellowship of the Blood-washed spirits and the holy angels of Heaven.

How, then, can we turn this privilege to the greatest advantage? Ah, that is an important question. The duty of aiming at it lies upon every Salvationist. Even the children can have a hand in it, and, oh, if everyone were to join in the attempt, what a wave of blessing would follow! If every officer were to become a member of my Profitable Conversation League, what useful and interesting talks there would be when officers meet, in their visitation, and in their fellowship with their soldiers! If every soldier also would join, what beautiful talks there would be at the tables, at the family gatherings, and the journeyings to and fro in their efforts to benefit the people!

IV

Well, let us inquire how this is to be carried out:

Watchfulness will be necessary. There should be a set purpose to guard and guide the tongue. The holy Christians of old used to talk about the grace of "Recollectedness"—that is, a state of mind which, so to speak, keeps the soul awake to the fact of who you are, and what you are doing, the opportunities of the occasion, and how you can best improve them. Oh, how often, after the event, do we say to ourselves, "Why did I allow that conversation to take that useless turn? Why did I not make an effort to turn it to better account? Or why did I not say something that would have been useful to A, or B, or C? Or why did I not propose a song, or offer to pray, or do something that might have been a blessing?"

But, alas! what is called our presence of mind—by which, I suppose, is meant recollectedness—as to who we are and what would be most likely to be useful at the moment—is too often wanting, and we lose the chance forever.

We Must Watch

Now, if we are to make the most of conversations, we must watch, and enter upon them as a duty, with a steady aim to make the most we can of them for God and for the well-being of those around us. Why not? A Salvationist goes to the open-air, or on to the platform, with such an object. He says to himself, "I am not going to let this meeting drift into a mere pastime, a thing for the amusement of the hour. No, I will, if I can, make it a benefit to someone for this world and the next." Why should there not be some similar resolution and purpose with respect to the innumerable opportunities of usefulness presented by conversation?

I specially want it to be seen that I am not advocating anything like bondage, of sanctimonious, or melancholy talk. Ah, no! Anything of the kind would defeat at once the object for which I am driving. For instance, only let the mother and the children feel, when they meet for the morning meal, that father will make it the opportunity for delivering some sort of a sermon, however important or ably it may be done, and farewell to the sort of conversation I mean. No, I would not, except under extraordinary circumstances, even recommend the mentioning of any theme to be talked over. Matters enough are always happening in connection with every household, every barracks, every community, and every nation to interest all, and which can be referred to, and turned to profit and made to instruct and interest everybody present, by a little contrivance.

Profitable Conversation

The same thing applies to the casual meeting of comrades, or, indeed, of anyone, where there is time for a little talk. The first condition of profitable conversation especially in the family or similar circles, is the sense of freedom. This necessitates a certain amount of what might be termed small talk, which more or less embraces the little matters that have to do with family and every-day life—chat about the health of all, the last letters from loved relations and friends, the sayings and doings of the children, their lessons, their toys and their play, the happenings at the meeting of the night before, the coming holidays, the weather, and a hundred other things are of overwhelming interest at the moment, and cannot be ignored. Indeed, if for no other reason, or carrying with them no other benefit, they serve to train the junior members of the circle in the art of friendly and polite conversation. Yet, after all or a portion of these matters have been turned over, more important subjects can be mentioned, and occasionally occupy the larger part of the time.

But with all the freedom and cheerfulness I have referred to, nothing should be said or hinted at which unjustly reflects upon the absent, or which is contrary to perfect love. How often, in the very height of that freedom and pleasantness, engendered by the interchange of thought and feeling which takes place in a conversation, does one of the twin serpents of envy and jealousy raise its hideous head and insert its venomous insinuations or deprecations, regarding comrades or friends! Oh, this thing must be watched and guarded against! And even when words of condemnation concerning either the present or the absent have to be spoken, they should be dipped in honey, and uttered with tenderness, for nothing is more calculated to put an end to the freedom of happiness of a talk than anything which approaches to bitterness, however necessary the saying of it may appear to be.

V
What Can Be Done?

What can be done, then to accomplish all this—that is, to make conversation as useful as possible?

1. Make a definite effort by starting topics that you can see will be interesting and useful to the company in which you find yourself, and, having started the conversation, try to keep it going. That is the difficulty. For myself, I have never failed to introduce a subject, but to keep it afloat has occasionally been impossible. The excitement arising from the meeting with friends seems to generate a kind of wordy mood that, unless taken hold of with a very strong hand, carries everybody away in any direction in which the wind may seem to blow, so that before one knows where he is, the topic he has brought on to the board has van-

ished, and three or four others are being discussed with great energy.

It is not a bad plan to have a little conspiracy among one or two members of the company to keep a given topic to the front. It can easily be done at the moment, and what one says the other can second or reply to, or raise a difficulty about, until all are interested, and then the ball will roll on of its own momentum.

2. Intelligent and interested listening has much to do with good talking. Who can talk when hearers make it evident that they are too impatient to listen, or that the time is all for themselves? I have found the greatest difference in the ease of difficulty with which I have commenced talking with those who pass for being the great people of the world. The manner of some men seems to stop the flow of my thoughts and freeze up my power of utterance, while that of others has had just the contrary effect, making it not only a delight to listen to their observations, but a pleasure to answer them, or to start off on a line of my own. You will have similar experiences in ordinary conversation. I meet so frequently with men and women who, sitting by my side, make it so evident that they care not for anything I can say, although it may concern matters as important as life, and death, Heaven and Hell, that I instinctively close up and retire within myself, like that snail into his shell, concluding, as I am often all but forced to do, that either I have nothing to say worth saying, or that my manner of saying it is without the power to charm. Others, however, will incline their ears, and answer me by approving nods, smiles, ejaculations, responses, and confirmatory expressions, which make it difficult for me to stop speaking or to tear myself away from their society. You will find it the same.

3. Encourage others around you to talk. Often those who have that to say which is worth saying will be the last to join in the general talk, while those who have the least matter will make the most rattle. Ask for opinions from the silent ones, in fact, it will be found not to be a bad plan to get everyone to give their own view of the subject. Don't overlook the women who may be present. How coolly and unjustly and thoughtlessly— I was going to say how conceitedly—the men will ignore the women when taking part in a conversation concerning a matter about which they have just as true, and perhaps even a more correct—and very often a more practical—judgment than themselves! They may not prohibit them

joining in the general talk—on the contrary, they may say that they have the same opportunity of expressing their opinion as the men—but the arbitrary manner in which they absorb the time, and address themselves to each other, makes it plain enough that they do not anticipate the sisters having anything worth saying upon the matter.

In the family, I need not point out that the mother ought always to have the opportunity, whether she uses it or not, of having her fair share in whatever conversation goes on, and on many questions it will not only be safe, but useful, and often very interesting, to bring the children in. It will make them listen to what their elders say, and help them, in forming habits of thought and expression, to deliver themselves, of their opinions before father, mother, brothers, and sisters.

4. Again, in conversation there should be nothing vulgar or unclean. I leave the family out here, considering such a thing to be impossible there, and speak particularly of talks when only men are present—although I am not sure how far women may occasionally err in this direction. Oh, how ready is the poor human heart to take fire! A very small spark may kindle a flame of lust that shall never be extinguished, no, not in the fires of Hell. I could not allow myself even to imagine that a Salvationist should lend himself to the expressions and anecdotes that pass current so freely amongst many ungodly men, nevertheless, I am quite aware that comrades may be betrayed into sayings that have double meanings, and that are not in keeping with the purity of heart enjoined by our Lord, and in which the Salvation Army glories.

VI
Beware of False Doctrine

5. Nothing should be allowed that is contrary to sound doctrine. If you have difficulties about the holy truths to which we stand pledged, leave them over until you come to know the will of God more perfectly. Remember how possible it is for you to instill doubts and the beginnings of unbelief in certain doctrines into the young and the ignorant, that shall go on fermenting and growing until they become roots of poison-trees that fill the soul and ruin the future life. You may be able to grapple with these infidel difficulties yourself, and emancipate yourself from them, but the hearts in which you sow the seed may not be strong enough to

accomplish this mastery, and consequently may go down under them forever. To show off your knowledge of evil might be an amusement to you, but prove death to those on whom you operate by your bit of knowledge. Beware!

6. Let there be no disloyalty. The shortcomings, misdoings and imperfections of those whom the providence of God has placed over you, is a tempting topic. False, fickle and weakly minds are only too often led away by it, and a heap of miseries and misfortunes follow. In the history of all organizations or governments, there have ever been men, and some women, who have delighted in destroying the confidence of the ill-informed and simple in the beneficence and rectitude of the governing powers, and that they will tell you without any evil intention. But, alas! evil consequences have followed, whether intended or no. Don't be one of these sneaking whisperers! Don't permit yourselves in insinuations in the dark, or suggestions wrapped up in smooth phrases, which you would be ashamed to have repeated in broad daylight in the hearing of those whose power for usefulness you seek, behind their backs, to cripple.

Be Loyal

I need not say that this refers to all classes of authorities—masters, mistresses, in the family, the workshop, Captains and Captains' wives, indeed, right up to the top, both in the Army and in the state. Neither practice, nor allow it, I say, in any company where you have a voice, or are present.

7. Keep as far off the dictatorial as you can. Don't speak in tones or with manners that would seem to imply that you are infallible, and that wisdom will die with you. Perhaps you may have some reason for entertaining the idea that you are in every way the superior in sense, intelligence and religion to those around you, and your notion may be a correct one, but that does not say that you should let everyone present see that you think so. Blessed are the meek, for they shall inherit, among other things, the kindly esteem of those with whom they associate, while the overbearing and masterful earn their hearty dislike, if not their absolute scorn.

23

Trade

SOME OF MY READERS will doubtless be engaged in trade, either as shop-keepers, factory owners, mechanics, farmers, or in some other class of business which will devolve upon them the duty of buying and selling goods of various description.

So that I do not feel that I can pass by the subject, and yet, I must say that I am not very confident that anything I can write will exercise any wide influence upon the matter. However, I will venture a few counsels, and will try and make them—as we sometimes say with respect to our talking—short and to the point.

I
Counsels

My first piece of advice to the tradesman, whosoever you may be, or whatever business you may have started, or be contemplating starting, is:

1. Do not have anything to do with any form of trade on which you cannot ask, and expect to receive, the blessing of Almighty God. That will shut you out of any kind of business that is based upon injustice or falsehood, or which can only prosper by trespassing upon the interests of your fellowmen. God is just, God is truth, God is benevolent, and you cannot expect him to give his approval or bestow his blessing on a trade or profession that is unjust in its character, which violates the principle of truth in its maintenance, or which can only succeed by inflicting injury on those whom he loves. You might as well expect him to bless and prosper the work of the devil as to do anything of the kind.

A Test Question

When, therefore, you are considering a trade for yourself or your children, ask yourself the question: "Can I stand in this shop, or go about these fields, or manage this factory, and do my buying and selling, as truly in the spirit of prayer and faith as I take my place in the open air, or stand up to give my testimony in the barracks? If not, I will have nothing to do with it."

I know that such a resolution, or the carrying out of such advice, will shut you out of many trades and professions as they are conducted in the present day. In conversation on the character of the different commercial and business methods now prevalent, a gentleman said to me a little time back: "I have had great experience in different countries in the way of business, and exceptional opportunities for judging the character of the methods that prevail with those engaged in its direction, and I have come to the conclusion that there is no trade or profession that is not dependent for its existence and prosperity, more or less, on fraud and falsehood." That was a sweeping charge, but he was a thoughtful, and I should think, a very trustworthy authority.

No Divorce of Religion from Business

Still, I think this gentleman's opinion was a great exaggeration. There must be a large number—may we not hope the majority?—of businesses whose directors, while not claiming to be actuated by religious principles, would scorn anything like willful injustice or positive misrepresentation. But then, there are many businesses, which, if not like the makers and sellers of intoxicants, whose fortunes are acquired in exchange for the bodies and souls of men, yet only live and thrive by ministering to the weaknesses, vices, and villainies of men. What Salvationist would like to earn a livelihood in such a fashion? Resolve, therefore, I say, that your business shall be a part of your Salvationism, and that you will have no trading concerns, however promising of money or anything else they may be, that will prevent you being as religious on Monday as on Sunday, and as prayerful and believing in trade as you are in your barracks.

2. Be just—that is, truthful, honest, and honorable in all your business

transactions. Be truthful, as good as your word. If people find that they can rely upon your word about the things you sell or the work you do, if they find that you are upright, and do not cheat and deceive them, that you are honorable, and do not take advantage of their ignorance, they will be pleased to have dealings with you, and will recommend their neighbors and friends to do the same. Honesty, in both word and deed, has usually been found to be the best policy in the long run, and if it does not pay so far as this world goes, your Heavenly Father will see that it does in the next.

The Blessing of Doing Right

What I have said in a previous paper about doing good work, I recommend to the consideration of all who may be either engaged in business or contemplate entering upon it. The advice then given simply comes to this: "Do the right thing in your trade transactions, whether it is profitable or otherwise, and always do it." Do right if the heavens fall, do right and prosper. Refuse to do it and perish, though all the inhabitants of earth and Hell unitedly swear to the contrary.

If people ask you if your prints will keep their colors in washing, and you know they will not, tell them so. If they are buying eatables, or medicines, thinking that they are pure, when you know that they are not, tell them that the articles are adulterated. If you are selling a horse that has a blemish, point it out to your customer, whether he buys the animal or not is not your responsibility, but you are responsible for doing right and thereby keeping clear of sin, and John tells us that "All unrighteousness is sin." What is the consequence of selling or not selling your horse in comparison with going to bed with that sin upon your conscience, or waking up in the middle of the night to find the bony fingers of Death gathering up your heartstrings, in order that he may carry you away to the great white throne to answer for that deception?

II

3. Beware of covetousness. By which I understand not only the desiring of other people's possessions, to which you have no right, but the longing after, the desire for, wealth, houses, lands, trade, or earthly things

in general for their own sake. It cannot be wrong to desire, and scheme, and toil for what are known as the necessaries of life, either for ourselves, for those dependent upon us, or for those whose miseries constitute their only claim upon our assistance. We are sure that it is right and commendable to desire, with all our strength, the gifts and graces of God's Holy Spirit. For this we have the authority of the apostle, who tells us to "covet earnestly the best gifts."

But, having food and raiment, and yet be everlastingly yearning after more of the world's riches is evil, and only evil, and evil continually. The love of money, which must include the kindred things that money represents, is, says Paul, "the root of all evil," being the baldest form of selfishness of which we have any knowledge. We see it displayed, in its beginnings, in the children, before they have learned to distinguish good from evil. Take that babe in its mother's arms, there are two apples on the table, and you give it one, which is as much as its little hand will carry, but it will want the other—that is, it covets. It cares not that its elder sister wants it, has a right to it, nay, maybe dying for it, all it knows is that the apple is there, it looks enticing, the child would like to have it, and therefore desires it.

That is covetousness in the child, but when we come to its grownup brothers and sisters, we find a covetousness much more hateful and injurious. We find them, while possessed of the one apple, desiring the other also, although they may know, which the child does not, that their elder sister will suffer, may perhaps die, in consequence.

Beware! Beware! Beware!

Beware of covetousness! God forbids it. He hates it. "Thou shalt not covet" is one of the great commandments of God.

Beware of covetousness! It is the author of endless heart-burnings, starvations, seductions, adulteries, suicides, and every other form of human misery. And among these miseries there stands out prominently the ruinous competition, the abominable slaveries and sweatings, so common in our day. "More business, and more business still!" is the cry, to gain which we must rob our neighbor of his customers by under-selling him, and in order to produce our goods at a lower price, we must pay less wages. The neighbor, not willing to be beaten, and determined to keep his trade, and even get more, reduces prices again, and so the game of beggar-my-neighbor, and especially beggar the poor wretches who have to stitch, stitch, stitch from morning till night, goes on. For all this, covetousness is, at the bottom, largely responsible. Oh, my friends, having food and raiment, cannot you learn therewith to be content?

Beware of covetousness! It makes a hell of the human breast. Our Lord said: "Blessed are they which do hunger and thirst after righteousness, for they shall be filled"—satisfied. It might with truth be written: "Cursed are they which do with covetous eyes hunger and thirst after the gold, and the silver, and the gains, and the praise, of this life, for the more they secure, the emptier shall they feel themselves to be, and the more they eat and drink of them, the further shall they be from satisfaction." Nay, not only so, but the very desire shall harden their hearts and destroy what there was of the kindly, and generous, and God-like in their manhood and womanhood, drying up the heart, and reducing them to mere things—machines—good for nothing, but, like the horseleech, to cry: "Give, give, give!" and feeling the worse rather than the better for what they get.

4. Deal in good and useful articles. Don't sell rubbish if you can help it. You act on the principle laid down in the barracks, and in your salvation business generally. If a man comes to buy the truth about God, and sin, and Heaven, and Hell, and Calvary, or any other aspect of your glorious salvation, you give him the unadulterated article. Do your business, comrades, whoever you may be, on the same line.

III

The early Quakers made a great name for themselves and piles of money by selling only first-class articles. At one time—not so very long ago either—if you wanted first-class clothes, or silks, or linens, or other things, you were sure of finding them at the shops of some of the old-fashioned Quakers, and perhaps there only in that city. It is true you had to pay for the article, but you got the quality for your money—and there are those who still maintain that good things are always the cheapest, even if you have to pay a high price for them. Anyway, our comrades, the Quakers, have found the plan to pay handsomely.

Trade on the Straight

Notwithstanding, acting on this advice will, I have no doubt, be found very difficult. To such heights of success has the vice of adulteration risen, that not only are buyers very much in the dark as to what they buy, but the sellers also as to what they sell. Anyway, be frank, I say, with your customers. If the articles are not likely to last forever and a day, you can, at least, be sure that their value is in proportion to the money paid for them—that is, that the purchasers have their money's worth.

And, after all, there is something to be said for what is, with much contumely, called the slop trade. What would the poor people do without it? There is the bespoke business for the West End, where money is no consideration, and there is the slop trade for the working-classes of the East, prices varying accordingly. The poor middle-woman is so wretchedly remunerated for her labor in the shirt-making line, that the poor man who has only sixpence in the world, and who is minus the usual underclothing, is benefitted thereby, seeing that he is enabled to secure a shirt for his sixpence. And although buying tea in pennyworths, instead of ordering it in the chest, is a most uneconomical way of conducting housekeeping, if the unfortunate creature has only a penny, give her a packet of the article for that amount—only see that she has all that can be afforded in quantity and quality for the money.

A Safe and Sound Maxim

5. Look after your own business. If you want a thing done well, do it yourself. I think that is a proverb, and if it is not, it ought to be. I am sure I have ever found it a safe rule of action myself. The officers in both the army and navy services are supposed, and that with good reason, to know most about the details of their position. They know what the work of the forecastle and the barrack-room is, because they have done it themselves. And no matter what trade a man may embark in, he should understand its inward workings. If not, he will be more or less at the mercy of other people, and they may not always guide him aright. Therefore, if you do not buy your goods, and serve your customers, and keep your books, and manage your stock-

taking, and do the whole round of your own business, see that you understand how it ought to be done, and so be able to direct others.

Workers and Shirkers

But next to doing your work yourself, with the natural interest which you are likely to feel in it, is the importance of seeing that it is done, and done properly, by other people.

Some men are a law unto themselves. They require no overlooker to be ever on their track to keep them up to the mark of duty. Rather are they like the willing horse, that, instead of whip or spur, has to be held back from doing more than his strength will allow. And not only is there the quality of labor, but the greatest care that it shall be done in the most efficient and profitable manner. But this class of servants is not too numerous. Nay, nay, there are still existent on the face of the earth a number of workmen and workwomen who do not answer to this description. On the contrary, they seem instinctively to shirk away their time, and shirk their work, or, at least, slur it over with little or no interest, and even less concern whether it is well done or not. These, for their own sakes, no less than for yours, require constant oversight. If you will look after them, point out their shortcomings, and urge them to better things, you may save them from drifting down to the lower depths and make them into good servants, nay, perhaps something higher in the social scale. If not, then they will possibly disappear from off the platform of respectable labor.

On the other hand, if you do not see, and that most carefully and constantly, that your work is done, done according to your wishes, and done well into the bargain, you may be pretty sure that your trading affairs will be liable to a not far-distant collapse.

My advice at this point of our subject amounts, in short, to this: Select your business carefully, start fair, with no impossible burden of debt, or rent, or interest on borrowed money, or heavy salaries of any kind. Plan with equal care how the business is to be carried on, and do the work yourself, if possible, or a good share of it. Choose the best helpers you can lay your hands upon to take your place, and then, with great care and undying patience, see that they carry out your plans, that is, do the work as you wish it done, and then it will be almost as good as doing it yourself—indeed, probably better.

IV

Look at the immense business establishments in our great cities. As I pass them by, and see the skill and industry manifested in the selection and endless variety of articles they keep for sale, the decoration of their buildings, the marvellous displays in their windows, the ceaseless ingenuity by which they keep themselves before the public and then go on to think of the talent required to manage their hundreds of employees, their finances, and I know not what, I am filled with wonder, and when I acquaint myself with the very ordinary abilities of the great bulk of the employees in these establishments, I wonder still more.

Brains to the Front

But the whole mystery is cleared up by the recollection, or the information, that out of the one thousand persons employed in the concern, there are ten, or perhaps twenty, really capable people, that these ten or more persons have contrived the business and started it off on its present line, that they select the goods, design the displays, suggest the advertisements, generally plan everything that is done, and see that the other 980 carry out their wishes, and who thereby serve the interests of the firm quite as well as if they were as clever as the twenty individuals with brains of whom I have spoken. They tell them what to do, and see that they do it.

Now, it is very improbable that any one of my readers should be contemplating an enterprise of the magnitude of the one of which I am speaking, or anything approaching to it, but however small the undertaking you may have in view, or under your hand, here are safe and sound principles on which you may conduct it, with a good promise of success:

Don't Live in a Fool's Paradise

6. Be careful to carry the correct knowledge of your financial position in your own mind. If you understand the proper method of keeping the

accounts of your business transactions, that will be good, very good—in which case you must keep them under your own eye if you do not do them yourself. Of course, I am only speaking of a small concern. If you do not understand bookkeeping, or if you have too large a business to do the work yourself, get some reliable person who is competent in that department. Anyway, you must know where you are all the time. Don't live in a fool's paradise, thinking you are doing a good thing, and getting a living, and making money into the bargain, when all the time you are going to the bad, living on your capital, and are on the downgrade which leads to the bankruptcy court.

7. Don't be over-sanguine. In the present age, with its enormous rents, and competition, and cutting prices, with its department stores—with all their advertisements and attractions—it is no easy matter for storekeepers to make a thing pay, and when you come to other kinds of trade, even the running of a laundry or a boot and shoe store, very much the same difficulties will be experienced. Therefore, if you want to prosper, go carefully, feel your way, and act with prudence.

Importance of Money Matters

8. Keep your expenditure down. It is much easier to spend than to make money. Do all the work you can yourself—that is the cheapest form of labor. Take an example from agriculture. A man, and his wife, and family, who work their own place will get a living out of ten acres, when another man, who has to pay for his labor, will starve on 5oo acres. There is a lesson in this for all sorts of tradesmen.

9. Make up your mind to have no debt, at least, no debt that will harass you or imperil your business. I have a great notion of a business done simply for cash, that is, when you pay cash for your goods, and only sell them for cash in return.

10. Beware of purchasing goods that you do not want, either because they are cheap, or to please those whose business it is to sell them. If you have not a ready market for them, don't have them, however far beneath their supposed value you may be able to secure them. If you have goods that are not saleable, get rid of them. Dead stock—that is, stock that does not sell—deteriorates rapidly in value. The fashion is ever changing, and even were that not so, the goods spoil as they lie upon your shelves. This

applies to almost every kind of commodity in the market.

11. If you keep assistants, deal wisely with them. Do so, even with the boy that sweeps your store, or takes down the shutters.

(a) Attach them to you. If they care for you and your concern, your interest will be theirs, and they will work for you more earnestly and efficiently than otherwise, and that at greater self-sacrifice, and for longer hours. Nothing can very well exceed the folly exhibited by many employers in the domineering, slave-driving manner with which they treat their servants. These employees either have hears, or they have not. If they are destitute of that organ—well, then, it will be quite consistent to treat them as the machines they would be, but if they have hearts, why not deal with them accordingly? They must do their work, and you must see that they do it, as we have already shown, but all and every direction given, and inspection made, can be done in the kindly spirit which will affect their hearts.

Making Good Servants

The old-fashioned servant, who spent his energies and years, and even laid down his life for his master and his master's family, is fast dying out, but you can create some more members of the fraternity, and that greatly to your own interest and their benefit.

(b) Attach them by instructing them. Give them every opportunity within your power of learning the business, whatever it may be.

(c) Encourage them. Beware of finding fault, until they lose heart and give up in despair.

(d) Devolve responsibility upon them as rapidly as they are deserving of it. There is nothing that develops ability, improves character, arouses ambition, and generally sets a man on to do the best he can for himself and those to whom he is accountable, like being made responsible for the discharge of some duty, the doing of which creditably will bring him praise, while the opposite will bring him blame.

(e) Make your helpers sharers in your prosperity, that is, let them benefit by your business in proportion to the profits made, if any. This will naturally make them more desirous than they otherwise would be that there should be profits to divide, and lead them out to more strenuous and self-denying effort to increase them.

V

Cooperation is an important feature in the spirit of the age. Amongst the moneyed classes its practice grows and thrives with remarkable rapidity. Syndicates and companies seem likely, in view of the immense amount of capital they can command, to absorb the business of the world, if they do not come to rule it. There really does not appear to be any limit to their future advances. Whether it is a just arrangement that men should, by clubbing their money together, overshadow and outdo their fellow tradesmen in the same line of things, I do not wait here to inquire, but, in view of the fact, it does seem to me to be desirable that laborers should combine after the same fashion. If 100 men, having $5,000 each, put it all into one pot, and by its means drive a powerful business along, why should not 1,000 men, able to scrape together $500 each, put this amount into a pot, and then, by this addition of their cooperated labor, make a large business, dividing the profits amongst them?

The scheme would be capable of any number of variations, and properly worked, could not fail, I should imagine, to be a great success, having in it the advantages flowing from the combination of capital, and the still greater and more efficient element of mutual interest in labor. Only two things would be necessary to that success. First, it must have in it the principle of true religion, and secondly, be conducted by a strong and just government.

The Spirit of Cooperation

Cooperation is founded on the spirit of justice. Those who do the work should have the gains. It will be said, in reply, that this is done, and often exceeded, in the wages paid. Quite true, but I think there should be a more direct connection.

Again, cooperation is the spirit of encouragement. We all know the difference in the results that flow out of what is called day-work and piece-work. When a worker knows that his wages are going to be a fixed quantity, regardless of the strength and ability he may put into his toil, he will be likely to be tempted to take it easy, whereas, if the returns are to be measured by the extent of his work, the effect will probably be the contrary.

Now, I am not advocating that you should at once start forth in the formation of a cooperative society, but suggesting that you should introduce this spirit into your business, whether large or small, by saying to your employees, many or few, "Now, while I propose to pay you a settled wage, I will give you, over and above that, a fixed percentage on all the profits that may be made." I think that such a course would not only be just, but very likely to encourage them to do all that in them lies to make it a growing success.

God's Share

12. Give to God the right and due proportion of your gains. In all the arrangements you make about your business, in all your plannings as to what you will buy, and sell, and how you will dispose of the profits you may obtain, be sure not to leave God out of your calculations. Do not attempt the experiment of dispensing with him, unless you want either the prosperity or the adversity that may attend your effort to prove your ruin, for if a man loses his soul as the result of his trading, it does not matter very much whether the ruin be brought about by one or the other. Therefore, I say, don't leave God out!

You must not only ask for his blessing and conduct your affairs in harmony with the principles he has laid down, but give him his share of the gains. Pay him his due, and pay him not merely in empty thanks and praises and adorations, nor even by asking him to save your soul from wickedness here, and to open the gates of Heaven to you hereafter. All that is very good, and beautiful, and necessary for you, but something more than that is required if you are, in only a very limited degree, to discharge the obligation under which you are laid to him for the services you expect him to render you. No, you must, among other methods, pay your debts in that form which is the most acceptable and appropriate to the occasion—that is, by giving him a fair share of your profits.

VI
The Tenth is a Practical Plan

But is not the notion of giving all you have to God also capable of abuse? Indeed, when you come to the practical application of the idea, does it not usually terminate in a dreamy sentimentalism? In the first place, the working of it out is impossible. It cannot, with the best intentions, be translated into fact. Take a man with a wife and five children, and an income of thirty shillings per week. If he literally acts upon this principle, he will give the whole thirty shillings, and have nothing left for the feeding, clothing, housing and all the other needs of his family! That would constitute his first duty. But it will be assumed that he must retain what, in his judgment, he feels to be necessary for those purposes—which is to say that he will probably retain all, or nearly all, of the thirty shillings, with which retention the giving of his all to God comes to an end.

Further, I have already said, and now repeat, that the giving of all in this literal sense usually leads to mere sentimentalism, neither useful to God nor man. I once knew a gentleman—and he is only an example of any number of the same class of people who have come under my observation—who was ever harping on the string that all he had was given to God, and yet he died leaving his family with nearly half-a-million of money.

Fix a Standard

No, I say, fix your standard at what you conscientiously feel to be the reasonable discharge of your duty in this respect. Begin, we will say, where God instructed Moses and his flock to begin—and they were poor enough in all conscience! That is, at the tithe. Lay aside a tenth of what you ascertain your gain to be, and give that to God. That will not prevent you going ahead of that amount. The Jew went far beyond it, for, in addition to the tithes, he had collections and donations in constant recurrence. Work out your rule on a graduated scale, beginning at the bottom with the tenth, and go on increasing the proportion as God shall increase your income. From a tenth you can rise to an eighth, and go on to a fifth, and even still further. Make his glory your joy, your conscience, your guide, and the salvation of men for time and eternity the supreme object for which you live, and trade, and everything else, and you will not go astray on this subject.

24

Poverty

MANY OF GOD'S PEOPLE are poor. God hath chosen the poor of this world to be rich in faith. For a long time in the early history of the church, poverty was a necessity. The man who embraced Christianity had to leave houses and lands, every door of business was closed to him, and no one would employ him, buy of him, or sell to him. The wilderness was his dwelling-place and the caves of the earth his home. His own family rose up against him, and cast him out.

Poverty is the lot of the majority of Christ's followers today. Only the poor will comply with the terms. It is still true. "How hardly shall they that have riches enter into the Kingdom of God!" They are called, but they will not comply. On the other hand, to many of God's children the avenues to profitable business are closed on account of conscientious scruples—they prefer poverty with a good conscience to wealth without it.

The Advantages of Poverty

Now, poverty is an evil, a part of the curse, the result of having to contend with "thorns and thistles." Still, it is not an unmixed evil. On the contrary, it has its compensations, or, rather its corresponding advantages. To begin with:

1. A poor man is more likely to be saved than a rich man. That is, he is more likely to listen to the call of mercy. A rich man will be contented with his lot. He will be so comfortable that he won't care about a change. The other will have less to give up, and will be the more ready to fall in with God's offer.

2. The pride of a rich man will make it more difficult for him to face the scorn that would come upon him from the world. The cross which a poor man has to carry is heavy enough, but that which a

wealthy person has to bear is often heavier, because it sometimes involves giving up his living, separating from well-to-do friends, or abandoning those social functions which he has hitherto been accustomed to.

3. Poverty is favorable to holy living. The same things in the lot of a rich man which makes his commencing a religious life more difficult than is the case with a poor man, are antagonistic to his attaining eminence in it.

4. Poverty is conducive to a life of usefulness.

Poverty and Greatness

5. Poverty has produced the greatest of the world's benefactors. The prophets of the old dispensation were nearly all poor. David began life as a plain, humble shepherd. Nehemiah, Daniel, and the three Hebrew children were all slaves. Elijah and Elisha were in a position answering to our Captains, without any D. O. to fall back upon when driven up in a corner. Isaiah, Jeremiah, Ezekiel, and the other prophets were all poor men and the children of poor men. Jesus Christ was a poor carpenter. All his apostles were, with perhaps one or two exceptions, the products of poor families.

If you come down to later times, the St. Franciscan and other orders who have at one time or another helped to save vital Christianity from extinction, have all been either poor in their parentage and breeding, or they have voluntarily made themselves poor for Christ's sake.

The Salvationists, with very few exceptions, have all been poor people, ignorant of the learning of the schools, or of the theology of the colleges. And yet they have done much to revolutionize the churches of the nineteenth century, and been the means of rescuing multitudes of the most hopeless sections of society.

If poor Salvation parents have their hands tied by their hardships, and are hindered from doing all that they themselves wish for God and souls, it is plain that they can produce giants, and rear heroes, out of their children, who will do wonders for their God and for the salvation of the world.

6. Poverty creates and encourages energy. Luxury and ease weaken and destroy those traits of character which make warriors.

7. Poverty is favorable to that sympathy and compassion which helps to make successful salvation soldiers.

Counsels

1. Praise God for the means you do possess. Look around you, and you will find any number of people who are far less favorably circumstanced than you are.

2. Remember that there is nothing in your lot to prevent you having the peace that passeth all understanding, and the joy that is unspeakable and full of glory.

3. If you have an opportunity of improving your circumstances, and, after prayer and reflection, you believe it to be in harmony with righteousness, and for the glory of God and the good of the Army, you are at liberty to embrace it.

4. If God prospers you, do not forget his goodness, grow proud, and cease to be the same humble, devoted, self-sacrificing salvation soldier that you were in the days of your hardship and poverty.

5. Whatever your lot, don't worry. Have faith in God!

25

Sickness

I HAVE ALREADY SAID something as to the value of health, and the importance of doing all that within us lies to maintain this boon. I do hope that my words, few and simple as they were, received due consideration, for we must all agree that prevention is better than cure.

But, for all that, sickness will intrude itself upon the best regulated families, and when the family is a pretty large one, it will seldom be absent for a very long time together. Therefore, perhaps no topic is much more important so far as this world goes, and perhaps no human knowledge has more to do with the peace, comfort, and general well-being of a household, than that which reveals the best methods of dealing with sickness when it does appear. What can I say? To begin with:

No Panic

1. Do not give way to unnecessary alarm on the first approach of sickness. Nothing will be more likely to effectually hinder your purpose of helping the suffering, than panic, or anything bordering upon it. Don't unduly magnify the matter, either to yourself or those around you, and especially would I say, "Do not affright the sufferer with any long faces about the seriousness of the afflictions."

The symptoms by which disease manifests itself may have a very strong resemblance in several different diseases. For instance, when we came to Fremantle, Western Australia, on my last visit there, it was found that we had a Sinhalese servant on board who had the symptoms of chickenpox upon him—which symptoms are very much like smallpox. The ship's doctor examined the man, and said he had chickenpox, but a Fremantle doctor, who was officer of health, said, "No, it was something more serious than that—it was smallpox," and as they did not want anyone to land with that disease, for fear of infecting the city, they sent fifty-two of the passengers into quarantine to wait and see if we had the disease as well. But, after waiting two or three days, the ship doctor turned out right, and the Fremantle officer of health proved wrong! It was not smallpox but chickenpox, and we were all set at liberty.

The Value of Hopefulness

Consequently, when several interpretations of the symptoms offer themselves—that is, when the heat of the skin, the pains in the head and back, and the general exhaustion, have the appearance of a bad feverish cold, or when they look like the beginning of influenza, or of some contagious fever—do not pounce down on the most dangerous disease of the three, but hope that it is nothing worse than the first and least serious. In following this course you can always encourage yourself with the saying of the man who affirmed that seven-eighths of the things that had given him the most trouble during his lifetime were those which had never happened. If applicable to anything in human history, I am sure that that is applicable to the anticipated afflictions of a family.

Anxious hearts are ever ready to fear the worst in such circumstances, especially when their loved ones are concerned. They cannot help it. Oh, how often, with my own dear children have I, at such hours, been able to calm the gloomy fears, and hush the anxious hearts to rest, by reckoning on the best, and my hopeful predictions have all but invariably turned out correct.

Precautions

2. But is it not the safest to always fear the worst and take precautions accordingly? Well, hoping for the best does not prevent such precautions being taken as would be called for in case of the worst. Often the simplest remedies prove the best in either case.

But is there not such a thing as losing time? Doubtless there is, and therefore every parent or person responsible for the health of others should be familiar with what may be termed serious symptoms, such as high temperature, a rapid or a slow pulse, prolonged retching, signs of delirium, persistent sore throat, long-continued sleeplessness, and so on.

3. When, however, there are good grounds for apprehending that the sickness is serious, means should at once be taken to get a satisfactory

and intelligent opinion as to the nature of the malady. In that direction, a doctor can help you, but even after you have called him in, and he has given his opinion, that should not prevent you exercising your own judgment, and carefully watching the progress of the case.

Doctors, Quacks, and Medicines

4. Beware of physics, whether it comes from a regular practitioner, or from that numerous body of professionals known as quacks, who pretend to cure everything with the same remedy. My own preferences are for what is known as the hydropathic system. I have seen in my own family in the days gone by, what might almost be styled miraculous cures, and strongly advise my readers to be at some trouble to make themselves acquainted with the system.

5. I recommended to the consideration of my comrades everywhere, old or young, male or female, what I have said on eating, drinking, clothing and the like, elsewhere in these chapters. Let them put those counsels into practice. There is a great deal in them that is applicable to what are called chronic diseases—that is, sicknesses that are of long duration, embracing disorders of the lungs or liver, the stomach and the like—and they will prove useful. For myself, when I get out of condition I usually fall back upon the fasting and extra sleep, with a little extra bathing. A lamp bath is a very common remedy, which opens the pores of my skin and induces perspiration, while a good rubbing will assist in putting me to sleep.

6. After all, the poor people must rely very much on the regular doctor. They are at his mercy, whether he belongs to the old, the new, or any other school. When I was sick in Australia, I felt so confused with the conflicting theories of the medical faculty, and so uncertain as to the possibility of finding anyone whose opinions would at all accord with mine, that I simply said, "Find, if you can, a capable, conscientious, and, if possible, a God-fearing man." They found me one, whom I believe answered to that description. As to the system that he followed, I am glad that I have not to pronounce an opinion upon it! I got well—that was what I wanted—and that quicker than anyone expected. He paid me every possible attention night and day, and would not receive any fee for either his medicine or trouble.

7. I need not impress upon Salvationists the duty of dealing faithfully with the souls of those by whose bedside they watch. If there is any uncertainty about their safety for eternity, push them up to that repentance and faith that will bring them peace in the cold river, and admission through the pearly gates into the City.

26

Bereavement

BY BEREAVEMENT I MEAN the loss of kindred, or precious friends, through death. To many of my readers this experience will be known as one of the most painful that comes to man. The loss of money, reputation, health, and a great many other losses, can be recovered, but the comrades of our hearts, and homes, and lives, when called away from earth, can never be restored to us in this world—they cannot be brought out of the grave, or given back to our fond embrace, until the resurrection morning. Death is a painful visitor. The poet sings:

> *Why do we mourn departing friends,*
> *Or shake at death's alarms?*
> *'Tis but the voice that Jesus sends*
> *To call them to his arms.*

That is beautiful, and as true as it is beautiful, nevertheless, after all has been said that can be said, to stand on the banks of the river and watch your best beloved go through its dark and stormy waters is a painful and agonizing experience.

I
The Spirit of Resignation

While conducting a series of Salvation meetings in a certain town and neighborhood, I once spent six weeks in the house of a friend. I thus had an opportunity of watching him very closely, and came to the conclusion that he was one of the holiest men it had ever been my privilege up to that time, to meet with. He has long since passed away to his reward, and I hope to meet him again, in the Gloryland.

This friend told me that he buried his first wife after they had lived together for but a very short time, that he loved her with all his heart, but that he was so filled with a sense of the rightness of God in taking her away, and so comforted by his presence in his soul, that had it been seemly he would have danced for joy at her grave.

Wesley sings of death in very much the same spirit. Here are a couple of verses:

> *Rejoice for a brother deceased,*
> *   Our loss is his infinite gain,*
> *A soul out of prison released,*
> *   And freed from his bodily chain.*
> *With songs let us follow his flight,*
> *   And mount with his spirit above,*
> *Escaped to the mansions of light,*
> *   And lodged in the Eden of love.*
>
> *Ah, lovely appearance of death!*
> *   What sight upon earth is so fair?*
> *Not all the gay pageants that breathe,*
> *   Can with a dead body compare,*
> *With solemn delight I survey*
> *   The corpse when the spirit is fled,*
> *In love with the beautiful clay,*
> *   And longing to lie in its stead.*

That sets forth an experience which, I confess, I have not been able to reach, and I fancy that many of my readers will be some distance from it. Although full of confidence as to the safety of their loved ones, their hearts will be more or less sorrowful at the trial they have been called to endure. What can I say to these sufferers?

The Spirit of Rebellion

1. Accept your life without murmuring. There is an important difference between being weighed down under the burden of the cross, and rebelling against it. To rebel against a divine decree will not help you.

One of my officers tells of a man who said he used to believe in God till he lost his child. When it died, he gave up the belief. The officer asked him whether his giving up his belief in God made him feel any better about the loss of his child? To rebel against the providence of God will only make matters worse.

2. Thank God for having favored you with such precious companions. Better to have loved, and been loved again, even though only for a short period, than never to have known such love at all.

3. Rejoice that your loved ones are safely landed on the eternal shore. If you had a son on the wide seas journeying to some distant land, and you received tidings that the vessel had struck upon some rock on a desolate coast, or been destroyed by fire in mid-ocean, your first inquiry would be, "What about the safety of the passengers? What about my son?" And if for a time you could gleam no information, you would be very much exercised. You would even go so far as to say, on the supposition that he had been drowned, that it would be a comfort to you if only his corpse could have been found and have received a decent burial.

But, suppose that unexpectedly the news reaches you, in the midst of your distress, that while the vessel was wrecked the young man was saved, and had been landed in a beautiful country, that he had started in an excellent business, that his health was good, his surroundings agreeable, with every prospect of his being well off, anyway for the rest of his life—how pleased you would be?

Now, all illustrations are poor indeed when you come to comparisons between earth and Heaven. But may not those whose dear ones have passed away from earth comfort themselves after the same fashion? They have suffered shipwreck—but they have not perished. No, they have been rescued, and carried off to a lovely land. Their wants are abundantly supplied, their companions are the Blood-washed multitudes and the holy angels, their employments will be pure and profitable, they will do the will of God and live in his presence forever, and know sin and sorrow no more.

II

4. Encourage yourself with the prospect of going to join them in that land to which your loved ones passed, and that before long. This was David's consolation on the loss of his child. He seems to have loved it very tenderly indeed, and there were few things in his kingdom that he would not have given to have kept it with him. But when it was gone, he bowed to the divine will, saying, "I shall go to him, but he shall not return to me."

Following up the illustration which I have already given you, on the news reaching the distressed father that his boy was safe, happy and prosperous, but so circumstanced as not to be able to return to his native land, or to again meet his dear father there, and, therefore, he had made arrangements by which both father and mother, and all his old associations, could come and live with him in comfort and harmony for the rest of their days, I think the parents and others who had loved the young man would be greatly comforted. I think his father would be likely to say, "Well, praise God! It is well with my boy, for although he cannot come to us, we can go to him. We may have to wait awhile, but we will surely go and see him again."

So, my comrades, your dear wife, or your husband, or your darling child—the flower of your flock—or some companion of your heart—a part of yourself, as it were—has suffered shipwreck on the ocean of time. Their vessel has gone to pieces, perhaps from old age, or, perhaps, it struck some sunken reef of fever or other disease, and went suddenly down. But your loved one is safe, manned by the angels, the life-boat came out from the golden shores and carried them safely into the desired haven. Already they are standing in the presence of the King, and not only so, but the message has come to you that arrangements have been made for your coming to share their happiness, and dwell with them forever.

Many years ago, I was much impressed by the following simple songs, and since then have been blessed many a time in singing them to myself. There may be some comfort in them to some of my readers, and although not original or unknown to many, I give them here for the benefit of those who have not met with them before. The first song is, of the saint:

I shine in the light of God,
His likeness stamps my brow,
Through the valley of death my feet have trod,
And I reign in Glory now.

I have reached the joys of Heaven,
I am one of the sainted band,
For my head a crown of gold is given,
And a harp is in my hand.

I have learnt the song they sing
Whom Jesus hath set free,
And the glorious walls of Heaven still ring
With my new-born melody.

Oh, friends of mortal years,
The trusted and the true!
Ye are watching still in the valley of tears
But I wait to welcome you.

Do I forget? Oh, no!
For memory's golden chain
Shall bind my heart to the hearts below,
Till they meet to touch again.

Each link is strong and bright,
And love's electric flame
Flows freely down like a river of light
To the world from whence I came.

Do you mourn when another star
Shines out from the glittering sky?
Do you weep when the raging voice of war
And the storms of conflict die?

Then why should your tears run down,
And your heart be sorely riven,
For another gem in the Savior's crown,
And another soul in Heaven?

But here I fancy some of my readers may be saying to me, "What if you cannot cherish this hope? We have been to the grave with those whose faith and character prevented us from having any such expectations as those you have mentioned, anyway, life is a dark uncertainty. What must we do? How can we comfort ourselves?" I can only make one reply: Leave them with God, and hope! The Judge of all the earth will do right. Hoping for the departed cannot do them harm. So exercise it, but let the uncertainty in which you are placed about the dead make you doubly diligent to do all that in you lies to secure a sure and certain hope for the living.

WILLIAM BOOTH

Minnie
Lindsay
Carpenter

William Booth
by
Minnie Lindsay Carpenter

The fascinating story of a great Christian soldier, and his struggle to build an army of Christian soldiers, to invade the world and save it from the flesh and the devil. Inspiring. (#1856)

Godliness
by
Catherine Booth

In spite of resistance from the church of her day, the Salvation Army's Catherine Booth was impelled to preach, and did so effectively that her appearance on a platform in London and throughout England was enough to fill meeting halls to capacity. An exceptional and rare compilation of her exhortations to a holy life. (#4219)